MW01025464

Roald Dahl

Roald Dahl

Teller of the Unexpected:
A Biography

Matthew Dennison

PEGASUS BOOKS
NEW YORK LONDON

ROALD DAHL

Pegasus Books, Ltd.
148 West 37th Street, 13th Floor
New York, NY 10018

Copyright © 2023 by Matthew Dennison

First Pegasus Books cloth edition January 2023

ISBN: 978-1-63936-332-2

10 9 8 7 6 5 4 3 2 1

Printed in the United States of America
Distributed by Simon & Schuster
www.pegasusbooks.com

'If you want a bar of chocolate, all you have to do
is go outside and get a bucket of mud.'

*Roald Dahl, explaining the workings of 'Bubbler's Instant Chocolate-
Making Machine' in notes for an unwritten story*

'Artists are not gods. They are entertainers, pure
and simple.'

Roald Dahl, letter to The Times, *7 February 1990*

'Give children well-bound books... Let them
have good illustrations and fine printing, and be full of
stories and tales of wonder. That done, have no fear that the
child will not learn to read. Children love to hear absurd
stories; you may see them every day in fits of laughter, or
shedding tears at what you tell them.'

Francois de Salignac de la Mothe-Fenelon,
On the Education of Daughters, *1688*

For Tom Cairns, in gratitude

Contents

Introduction

'A Perfectly Ordinary Fellow'

'I'M A PERFECTLY ordinary fellow, except that I happen to be very tall,' Roald Dahl told a group of children in 1975.[1] As with any number of pronouncements he made about himself over the course of an unpredictable life, he was aware of its disingenuousness even as he asserted its truth. Whatever his fictional stock-in-trade, Roald insisted, a writer seldom rivalled his characters for excitement: readers must not expect 'fiery eyes and a green moustache and ink all over [the writer's] clothes'; 'a writer, when you meet him, is not in the least bit like the books he writes'.

Really? At least we can agree that Roald Dahl was not a perfectly ordinary fellow. He was neither eager nor willing to be mistaken for such. Admittedly he lacked a green moustache, his dislike of male facial hair as studiedly intemperate as many of his foibles. But his belief in fantasy, grotesquerie, magic – the building blocks of so many of his fictions – ran deep, and the stark polarities of good and bad which shape his narratives reflected a black-and-white dichotomy within his own outlook that more than once proved detrimental to his happiness, wellbeing or reputation.

Like Beatrix Potter and Kenneth Grahame, whose lives I explored in short biographies in 2016 and 2018, Roald Dahl achieved extraordinary commercial success with work that has proved enduringly popular: paperback sales of *Charlie and the Chocolate Factory* and its sequel

Charlie and the Great Glass Elevator exceeded more than 4 million in the UK alone by the time of his death.[2] Beatrix Potter correctly predicted that her fame would rival Hans Christian Andersen's; Roald might have said something similar. Indeed, in 1988, withdrawing from a government committee examining schools' teaching of English, Roald justified his claim to omniscience in the matter of children's reading by referring Education Minister Kenneth Baker to his record-breaking sales figures. In more than three decades since his death, his books have continued to sell in remarkable quantities, milestones in the cultural landscapes of successive generations: celebrated, imitated and frequently adapted for stage, screen and radio. As he regarded himself, very tall Roald Dahl – writer and commercial commodity – is a giant.

He is also, as he was in his lifetime, a divisive figure. At its best, Roald's writing both for children and adults is lyrical, hilarious, vivid, unpredictable, tender and utterly absorbing; his darkest fictions portray without regret a world of cruelty, cynicism, misanthropy and caprice. In a story written for private circulation, P. L. Travers, creator of Mary Poppins, claimed 'Children have strong and deep emotions but no mechanism to deal with them.'[3] Time and again, Roald provided his underdog heroes with the mechanisms for dealing with these emotions and the circumstances from which they might emerge. Roald's detractors condemn bullying, vituperation, stridency, subversion and gratuitous scatology as characteristics of the man and his work. This Roald is coarse, misogynistic and an anti-Semite – for all his denials, anti-Semitism did shape aspects of Roald's thinking. Irascible, dominant and hectoring, he could be, as his three-year-old son described him, 'just a wasps' nest'.[4] Grounds for critic Kathryn Hughes's unsympathetic assessment of Roald as 'crashing through life like a big, bad child' are clear, but this is a selective view, countered by testimony to Roald's charm, kindness and generosity, and for the majority of his child readers what Hughes castigates as Roald's 'grandiosity, dishonesty, and spite' play no part in the writing that constitutes his continuing claim to our attention.[5]

In the second half of his life, with the success of his writing for children, beginning in the 1960s, Roald repeatedly spoke and wrote about his work and the qualities within him that he believed uniquely equipped him to satisfy his audience. He denied any purpose behind his writing beyond an evangelical zeal for turning children into readers. 'There are very few messages in these books of mine. They are there simply to turn the child into a reader of books. Damn it all, they are mostly pure fantasy,' he wrote to a linguistics student in 1989.[6] He told an American academic, to whom he refused assistance with the writing of his biography, to look for the material he needed in the books themselves: 'Your book, if you are going to do it, would have to be primarily based on your own analysis of my work, which is basically what all biographies are.'[7] In the present work, I have – up to a point – followed this testy injunction; I have given consideration to Roald's verdict that 'the things that go into [one's] books come from one's imagination – from a small secret part of the brain which is able to invent things and dream up funny stories' and his disclaimer that his books aim simply to entertain and engage.[8] The picture that emerges is of a man, like most of us, composed of contradictions, responsible for a body of exceptional story-telling – and often, as he described himself, 'a jokey sort of fellow [with a liking for] simple tricks and jokes and riddles and other childish things … unconventional and inventive', certainly not 'perfectly ordinary'.[9]

I

'LITTLE BOY BLUE'
1916–1930

'I do not remember much of it; not before anyway;
not until it happened.'

'I GOT IT ALL wrong,' commented Roald Dahl of his first draft of *Matilda*, his last full-length novel for children. He identified his mistakes in constructing his original story: 'The parents were normal. No good. The school was ordinary. No good.'[1]

Neither is a criticism that can be levelled at Roald Dahl's own childhood – parents or schooling. His enterprising father Harald was a perfectionist: exacting, undemonstrative (as Roald would prove), acquisitive but conscientious, the eldest child of an enormously tall, feckless Norwegian provincial butcher – like the husband in Roald's story 'Genesis and Catastrophe', 'an arrogant, overbearing, bullying ... drunkard'[2] – and, following bungled treatment of a teenage accident, an amputee, but shrewd, determined and, in time, rich. From his native Norway, intent on becoming an artist, Harald had travelled to Paris. From Paris he moved to the docklands of south Wales, in the late nineteenth century a centre for coal exports, dependent on Scandinavian timber for the pit props known as 'Norways'. There, some time in the 1890s, he set aside bohemianism. In Bute Street, Cardiff, with a distant kinsman and fellow Norwegian, Ludwig Aadnesen, he founded a company of shipbrokers that bore both their names, Aadnesen & Dahl. The process of personal reinvention was as thorough as ecdysis: enthusiastically Harald embraced commerce and

9

Britishness. In insular times, he retained aspects of an outsider's status, passed on in varying degrees to his family. All his children, including Roald, were baptized in the small white Norwegian church in Cardiff docks that still stands today, though religion scarcely touched their family life; throughout his childhood Roald held a Norwegian but not a British passport, and his first sentence, uttered at the age of two, was in Norwegian not English. Harald died in the spring of 1920, when Roald was three and a half. Weeks before, his eldest daughter Astri, 'far and away' his favourite child, had died at the young age of seven.[3] His shipbroking fortune amounted to £150,000, equivalent at current values to nearly £7 million, a more than comfortable nest egg for his grieving family. Among the death bed promises he extracted from his wife was an assurance that his children would be educated in England. Family tragedy – a father and sister lost – imprinted Roald's first horizons. From the outset his was not an ordinary childhood.

Among Harald Dahl's legacies to Roald were aesthetic sensibilities (carefully cultivated) and a love of nature; the 'many curious objects' that cluttered the table in Roald's writing hut as an adult included a silver and tortoiseshell paper knife of Harald's.[4] A conscientious philanthropist, in the winter of 1918 Harald had been listed among leading donors to a fund 'for the relief of distress' caused by Spanish flu in Cardiff; the following year, he had subscribed £25 to an appeal for a Welsh national war memorial.[5] Romantic for all his shrewdness, he had named his son after his hero, Norwegian explorer Roald Amundsen, the first man to reach the South Pole. Adventure and philanthropy would play their part in Roald's life, too. Harald had been married twice. His first wife, Marie Beaurrin-Gressier, died in 1907, leaving behind Roald's half-siblings, Ellen and Louis.

Any memory of Harald was overshadowed for Roald by his mother. Harald's second wife, Sofie Magdalene Hesselberg, was a stubborn, strong, private woman in her mid-thirties. In her children's assessment 'dauntless', 'practical and fearless', Sofie Magdalene was also Norwegian, by nature mystic, gossipy, occasionally impractical but without feyness, omnivorous in her curiosity about the world around her, the cornerstone and, as he remembered it, primary influence of Roald's fatherless boyhood.[6] On Harald's death, save her deathbed promise about schooling, she might have recrossed the North Sea to her homeland, taking with her Roald, his sisters Alfhild and Else, and her unborn child. Instead, the heavily pregnant widow stayed in south Wales, in the large farmhouse in Radyr, west of Cardiff, bought by Harald in 1917. In the autumn she gave birth to her last child, Asta. Like Mrs Fox in *Fantastic*

Mr Fox, she 'gathered her four children close to her and held them tight'.[7] Friendless but apparently unweeping, assisted by a Norwegian nanny called Birgit and comforted by busyness and a Pekinese (a breed Roald later disdained), Sofie Magdalene rooted herself in this alien landscape and the ugly house of tall chimneys and half-timbered dormers that Roald recalled as 'mighty … with turrets on its roof and with majestic lawns and terraces all around it', and, beyond, woodland, pasture, 'haymaking, hay wagons and horses' and, at harvest time, fields of corn stooks through which the children wandered at will; and dependents including 'a ploughman and a cowman and a couple of gardeners and all manner of servants in the house itself'.[8] 'She refused to take the easy way out,' Roald remembered: she was his first and, bar himself, most enduring hero.[9] (One of her granddaughters, by contrast, remembered her more ambiguously as 'the steely Norwegian widow'.)[10] To her children she spoke English as well as Norwegian, a factor in Roald's subsequent identity as 'very English, you know, born and bred, in spite of my name', 'an Englishman who lives in England'.[11] Undoubtedly, her stern lack of sentiment and physical reserve contributed to Roald's inability, regretted by his daughter Tessa, to express affection physically, the swiftness with which he became 'totally untactile'.[12]

Harald's will denied Sofie Magdalene financial independence. Its terms required her to seek authorization from her fellow trustees Ludvig Aadnesen and Harald's brother Oscar, who lived in France, even for nugatory expenses. Its effect was twofold: unnecessary complications, including sharp exchanges between Harald's widow, Aadnesen and Oscar Dahl, and a suggestion that there was less money than there undoubtedly was. Within a year, Sofie Magdalene had sold Ty Mynydd and its 150 acres, shearing herself of the burden of farm ownership. With her family of six, she returned to nearby village-like Llandaff – Roald's birthplace, on 13 September 1916, at Villa Marie, Fairwater Road. The Dahls' new home, Roald's third, was Cumberland Lodge, now a nursery school, smaller than Ty Mynydd. For Roald, looking back, it was 'nothing more than a pleasant medium-sized suburban villa': substantial, red brick and undistinguished, with large gardens of tall hedges, doily-patterned rosebeds, cricket nets.[13] He omits – because he took them for granted – mention of the house's many books or the clutch of garden buildings in which the children played unsupervised. Before his fifth birthday Roald had lost father, sister and a small boy's Eden of wide-open spaces, cattle, horses, pigs and chickens; in their wake vanished some of the easy certainties of conventional middle-class childhood. Of the children who people his novels, none possesses two loving parents and material security, or enjoys unchallenged the freewheeling joys of country life that always delighted Roald. Although Roald was too young to notice it, his father's death also loosened the family's rootedness in Wales. By choice, Harald had established his business in Cardiff. With her children and stepchildren, Sofie Magdalene remained in Llandaff, in the north of the city, until 1927, when she moved to Bexley in Kent. Her engagement with the country of her short marriage was circumscribed. Every Easter, she took a rented house in the Old Harbour at Tenby. There, the steep cliffs and Caldy Island a boat ride away offered seabirds' nests for plunder for the collection of birds' eggs Roald housed in wooden drawers lined with pink cotton wool; he climbed with a teaspoon in his pocket, using this to lift the eggs, 'so as not to leave the human finger smell behind on the other eggs because this might make the mother desert'; on Caldy Island cliffs his prizes included a guillemot's egg.[14] Instead Sofie Magdalene's outlook was by turns Scandinavian and Anglocentric: she read Ibsen, Knut Hamsun and Sigrid Undset, and Galsworthy, Bennett and Kipling; Hardy and Chesterton were her favourites. Roald's 'insider/outsider' status – a wealthy non-Briton, born in Wales of Norwegian parents, mostly educated in English preparatory and public schools, but fatherless – had deep roots. His repeated assertions of his 'Englishness' as an adult obscured ambivalence: contempt colours his description, for example, of the English upper middle classes, to which he appeared to belong, as 'smooth, well mannered, overweight, loud-voiced and infinitely dull'.[15]

The nameless boy narrator of *The Witches* is seven when a car crash kills both his parents. Roald was half this age when Harald Dahl died of pneumonia (and, possibly, following Astri's death from appendicitis, a broken heart). In the novel, the boy's grandmother hugs him through the first devastated night. Thereafter, 'in order that we might both try to forget our great sadness, [she] started telling me stories'.[16] Dahl family legend invests Sofie Magdalene with a similar role. In place of easy embraces, she distracted her children with tales, 'Norwegian stories ... to do with trolls and the dark winters', and a rosy account of Harald; Roald remembered her as 'a great teller of tales' to whom her children listened enthralled.[17] Did it work? Roald would almost certainly have argued that he survived because children are shaped for survival. For her part, total absorption in her role as mother – 'the matriarch, the materfamilias', as Roald described her – gave a purpose to Sofie Magdalene's own continuance.[18] With good reason, Roald suspected the element of need in his mother's wholehearted focus on her offspring, something approaching 'the deep conscious knowing that there was nothing else to live for except this' that he attributes to a doting mother in an early short story.[19] Her response spawned other consequences. Storytelling, especially about their own family, became integral to her relationship with Roald. Sofie Magdalene's determination to keep Harald alive for Roald made mother and son conspirators in a partial fiction on which, in the short term, both depended; stories – which demand the listener's imaginative engagement for their reality – played their part in ordering Roald's world. From his first separation from Sofie Magdalene, at preparatory school, Roald in turn made use of vivid anecdotes and commentary boisterously laced with slang to construct a part-fictionalized version of himself intended to reassure his mother and, in a pose of indomitability to which he would resort lifelong, bolster himself. His relationship with Sofie Magdalene was the closest of Roald's childhood. His sisters considered them remarkably alike.[20] Alfhild remembered Roald as 'what we called the apple of her [Sofie Magdalene's] eye. We always teased him, he was known as "the Apple".[21] Semi-truths, like Sofie Magdalene's 'Harald', forged a pattern for Roald's remembering – unapologetically, he excused himself later as merely making 'the Truth a little more interesting'.[22] A part of him would continue to claim for himself the role of 'apple' in key relationships. In his family life, he never willingly forfeited the status of pivotal male – Harald's by right – thrust upon him from childhood.

Else described the Norwegian folklore to which Sofie Magdalene introduced her children as 'peculiar [and] sort of morbid', 'all about witches, for Norway, with its black forests and icy mountains, is where the first witches came from', or like the shadowy stories of the recently deceased Jonas Lie, based on the legends of Norway's north-western province of Nordland, which Roald continued to admire: a portrait of Lie hung in the sitting room of Gipsy House, Roald's home from 1954.[23] She recited nursery rhymes, which delighted Roald, especially his favourite, 'Little Boy Blue', with its sheep and cows and meadow of haystacks, like his first memories of Ty Mynydd; as an adult he rewrote a selection in characteristically mischievous vein, including 'Hey diddle diddle' and 'I had a little nut tree'. At school, Roald wrote a spirited defence of nursery rhymes' 'concise description of a simple thing, leaving a vivid picture … in the memory of the reader', a technique at which he himself came to excel; he argued for a link between early exposure to nursery rhymes and imagination. Confronted by a grandfather clock, suggested the teenage Roald, the child who has learned nursery rhymes 'weaves a halo of romance' around it. 'Shivering with excitement', he or she peeps inside the clock in the hope of glimpsing the mouse they have heard about in 'Hickory, Dickory Dock'. The non-learner of rhymes, by contrast, grows up to be a non-reader, always for Roald an indictment: 'the sort of person who simply cannot think of what there is to say at a tea party'.[24]

As a writer for adults and children, Roald Dahl conjures worlds in which men and women, boys and girls frequently 'shiver with excitement'; his narrators delight in spying out mice inside metaphorical clocks. All too often excitement gives way to catastrophe, like the joyful new parents shot by New York policemen in a short story called 'Pig', or gluttonous Augustus Gloop confronted by a river of chocolate in *Charlie and the Chocolate Factory* and, with dire consequences, 'deaf to everything except the call of his enormous stomach'.[25] In every case, as Roald's readers learn quickly, excitement's coda is unexpected. This swiftness of reversal is central to his plotting and the stories' world view. Personal experience, beginning with the unremembered traumas of his father and sister's deaths, would convince Roald of the ubiquity of caprice in human lives. Nursery rhymes, fairytales and folklore provided his first introduction to unanticipated, frequently fearsome outcomes, tropes that played their part in shaping his fictional vision.

Like other authors of children's fiction, Roald prided himself on the vividness of his childhood recall.

Remembering was selective. An entry he would make in one of the writer's notebooks he called his 'ideas books' for 'a story with a young child and his thoughts' points to his conviction, even before he began writing for children, that he could reconnect with his own former thoughts; with the exception of *Esio Trot*, his stories for younger readers employ a double narrative perspective, balancing a child's thoughts with Roald's own adult outlook.[26] Yet of the experience of Elm Tree House kindergarten, close to Cumberland Lodge in Llandaff, beginning when he was six, Roald remembered little: the excitement of his journey there by tricycle with Alfhild, pedalling too quickly on the empty roads of the 1920s, leaning sharp into corners, balancing on two wheels; and, less appealingly, since neither Sofie Magdalene nor Birgit had taught him to read, the forty minutes he stayed behind each afternoon 'for extra lessons in reading because I was so backward', and the fear that followed, returning home on winter afternoons, of the black trees that overhung dark lanes, rustling in invisible winds.[27] With the exception of Matilda Wormwood, the five-year-old prodigy in *Matilda*, Roald's child heroes are at least seven, the age at which his own sharpest recollections began. His clearest early memories were of an ex-miner called Jones. Known to Roald and his sisters as 'Joss Spivvis', Jones was 'a short, broad-shouldered, middle-aged Welshman with a pale brown moustache' employed by Sofie Magdalene as a gardener.[28] A shared enthusiasm for Cardiff City football club and, in Roald's case, hero worship, sealed their friendship: Jones's account of rescuing his pit pony from an escape of flammable gas when he was eleven thrilled his boy-listener. Six days out of seven, in the musty privacy of the Cumberland Lodge tackroom, gardener and boy shared the lunch prepared for them by Mrs Jones: four buttered Crawford's crackers each 'and two large hunks of Cheddar cheese'. Roald used his penknife to slice the cheese, copying Jones. He 'perched on a sack of maize or a bale of straw while Joss sat rather grandly in an old kitchen chair that had arms on it'.[29] 'Endless' were the stories the Welshman told his acolyte in their shared male sanctums of tackroom and potting shed.[30] Private enclosures full of storytelling would feature prominently in Roald's life.

The versions of his memories that Roald preserved in his ideas books, in his extensive notes on writing for children and in autobiographical work like *Boy* and *Memories with Food at Gipsy House* suggest an upbringing marked by the same oscillations of wonder and alarm, excitement and boredom, fear and self-dramatization that crisscross the majority of childhoods. (In Roald's case, the sense of wonder, along with the self-dramatizing impulse, persisted, and his contemporaries considered that his family circumstances added up to 'an unhappy early life'.)[31] 'I know that young people have just as many worries as grown-ups,' Roald wrote as an adult. He recorded his response, aged eight, to a clockwork motorboat bath toy that sank after developing a leak: 'For many weeks after that, I would lie in my bath worrying about whether my own skin would develop a leak in it just as the little boat's had done, and I felt certain my body would fill with water and I would sink or die. But it never happened and I marvelled at the watertightness of the skin that covered my body.'[32] The older Roald takes seriously his child-self's certainty of fatal waterlogging: he makes clear that his 'worrying' overshadowed subsequent marvelling. This empathy with a child's conviction of vulnerability splices all his stories of children pitted against horrible grown-ups: it is the quality in his fiction that has convinced generations of child readers that, in a world of adult menace, the author is on their side. That the child ricochets so swiftly from terror to ecstasy, anxiety to reassurance, collapse to exultation, in no way diminishes the acuteness of his or her fear, Roald understood. His understanding was grounded in remembering.

To Roald, it was natural that each summer Sofie Magdalene took her children to Norway. He described it as 'like going home': 'We all spoke Norwegian and all our relations lived over there.'[33] Only later did he sense the chilly torpor of his grandparents' house in Oslo's Josefines Gate, with its large, heavily curtained rooms like those inhabited by the narrator's grandmother in *The Witches*: eventually, he recognized it as the 'quiet, gloomy ... neat and polished' backdrop to the lifelong imprisonment of his spinster aunts, Ellen and Astri, prevented by their father's force of will from marrying or leaving home.[34] In the short term, it was the scene of affectionate embraces and celebratory feasts, culminating in 'tremendous craggy mountain[s] of home-made ice-cream', and reached only after days of travel: trains from Wales to London and London to Newcastle, followed by a stomach-lurching two-day ferry shunt to the Norwegian capital, known until 1925 as Christiania.[35] In *Boy*, Roald's novel-length account of his childhood, Dahl's grandparents – 'Bestepapa' and 'Bestemama' – are figures of children's fiction, white-haired and wrinkled, his grandmother in a rocking chair, his grandfather smoking a clay pipe. Their encounters were brief, lasting no more than half a day, dominated by the set-piece splendid lunch, complete with Norwegian-style toasts and salutations. Grandparents are significant in Roald's children's fiction; he saw little of his own. Those impressions he did retain were coloured by memories of food and the excitement of the family caravanserai: Sofie Magdalene, her children, stepchildren, their nanny and an extra friend each for Ellen and Louis, a party that required three taxis for the connecting journeys from railway stations to docks, Josefines Gate and Oslo's Grand Hotel.

After the Hesselberg house, the final destination for mother, nanny, six children and add-ons was the island of Tjome, a day-long steamer trip across the Oslo-fjord. This last watery passage signalled the holidays proper, a crossing from the everyday to the fantastical. Again it was enlivened by Sofie Magdalene's storytelling – steeping her children in myths of the seas and mountains and the 'swirling mists and ghostly vapours' that Roald recycled as Dream Country in *The BFG*, making up new stories and retelling the popular, Grimm-inspired folk tales of Norwegian authors Asbjørnsen and Moe, including 'The Three Billy Goats Gruff' and 'The Giant Who Had No Heart in His Body' – as well as by her exploits that, in Roald's accounts, were intrepid, exhilarating, heroic: in a temperamental motorboat in open water, cleaving towering waves in pursuit of deserted islands for bathing and picnics, Sofie Magdalene imperturbable at the tiller, her children without lifejackets clinging to the boat's sides, and Nanny praying for safety, while the white-painted craft dramatically plunged and soared. Roald called Tjome 'the magic island'; he remembered it as 'the greatest place on earth'.[36] His ingredients for 'the perfect life for a small boy', described in *James and the Giant Peach* – 'a beautiful house beside the sea … plenty of other children for him to play with … the sandy beach for him to run about on, and the ocean to paddle in' – resemble those of his own childhood holidays.[37] 'What a child wants *and deserves* is a parent who is sparky,' Roald insisted in *Danny the Champion of the World*.[38] Sofie Magdalene's sparkiness was sealed for her son in those Norwegian summers of the 1920s, when, on the islands of the Oslo-fjord, she combined the roles of mother and father: energetic, brave, unselfish.

'I dreamed of an iceberg. It was a large iceberg, which floated lazily on a cold ocean, as if in sleep,' Roald wrote, in a teenage essay called 'Dreams'.[39] Within living memory was the sinking of the *Titanic*. In Tjome and the Oslo-fjord, the reality of icebergs was more vivid for Roald than for contemporaries raised on reports of nautical disaster. In Norway, the landscape of folklore merged with his surrounds; even the souvenirs Roald chose suggested a place wilder and untamed: a reindeer's antler paper knife, a toy seal made from seal skin. Annually, the magic island replaced the vanished idyll of Ty Mynydd: 'there were the wooden skeletons of shipwrecked boats … and wild raspberries, and mussels clinging to the rocks … and shaggy long-haired goats, and even sheep'.[40] At sunrise, as he wrote later, were 'bits of pale gold … flying among delicate, frosty-white flakes of cloud, and over to one side the rim of the morning sun ... coming up red as blood'; there were fairground rides in fishing villages, wooden roundabouts operated by hand.[41] In the summer of 1927, Roald found a chrysalis there; back at home, in a small pot in the garden, he waited for it to hatch.[42] Tjome dissolved the bounds between the visible and the fantastical, one source of the magic realism of Roald's writing.

In time, Norwegian summers offset the horror of Roald's school days. A century ago, boys' schools enmeshed their charges in vortices of rules and proscriptions, quick to punish, including canings and beatings, kindness at a premium. Roald's first experience of the 'English' schooling system so admired by Harald was the cathedral school in Llandaff, then in buildings close to the cathedral itself. It was the same school that Louis had attended, and convenient. Faithful to her husband's choice, Sofie Magdalene experienced few qualms transferring Roald from Elm Tree House. He would leave after only two years, in 1925, following corporal punishment so brutal that his mother withdrew him on principle. Her stand proved counter-productive. A reluctant solution on Sofie Magdalene's part, made under pressure from the family doctor, boarding school succeeded day school. St Peter's, Weston-super-Mare, across the Bristol Channel from Cardiff, emerges from Roald's accounts as joyless and brutish. Its headmaster set the template for Dahl teachers: a 'monster', 'beastly [and] cane-happy' – like Miss Trunchbull, who terrorizes Matilda, 'eccentric and bloodthirsty'.[43]

'I'm afraid I like strong contrasts,' explained Roald, at the end of his life. 'I like villains to be terrible and good people to be very good.'[44] He learned the starkness of the contrast between villainy and goodness at school. In the overwhelmingly female environment of Cumberland Lodge, Roald's special position as Sofie Magdalene's only son conferred privileged status. It did not take him long to discover that, at the all-boys St Peter's, his sex – along with every other pupil – indicated to a common room of First World War veterans an almost certain predisposition to wrongdoing. At home Roald was cheerfully unruly, energetic, independent. Exposure to Norse myths encouraged a relish for the cataclysmic. He disliked Arthur Ransome's *Swallows and Amazons*, for example, published when he was fourteen, on the grounds that it was 'too soft', but delighted in the grizzly didacticism of Hilaire Belloc's *Cautionary Tales*, which he had learned by heart by his ninth birthday.[45] Sometimes his derring-do involved his sisters: he padded Asta with cushions, then, to their shared delight, shot at her repeatedly with his air rifle, curious to see how far the pellets would penetrate. Sofie Magdalene's parenting was liberal, unconventional, even lax – she once told Roald his gym shoes 'smelt like a cat's crap' – but none of Roald's schools offered vents for high spirits.[46] A schism divided home and classroom. 'A foreigner [who] didn't understand how British schools were run' in Roald's version of his departure from the cathedral school, Sofie Magdalene had done little to prepare her 'Apple' for schools' pettifogging discipline, the 'rules and still more rules that had to be obeyed', the self-luxuriating regimentation against which Roald jibbed for the next decade and beyond.[47] How different it was from the rapscallion vim and excitement of life at Cumberland Lodge: Saturday football matches at Ninian Park with Spivvis and the comfortable fug of the tackroom or sheltering from the rain in the potting shed; taking pot shots at Asta; or the visit Roald made with Sofie Magdalene to the Lake District to visit Beatrix Potter's house.[48] In the garden, familiar from *The Tale of Jemima Puddleduck*, he glimpsed Potter herself.

It was a prank leading to a beating that brought about Roald's move to St Peter's, aged nine, in the autumn of 1925: Sofie Magdalene's horrified response to Roald's bruised and weal-striped bottom, after four strokes of the headmaster's cane. In *Boy*, Roald's retelling is in line with his views about writing for children. Its 'strong contrasts' are between his own haplessness and the dyed-in-the-wool nastiness of the story's villains: the hag-like owner of a sweet shop, Mrs

Pratchett, and the trigger-happy headmaster, Mr Coombes, repeatedly likened to a giant, 'well practised and [with] a splendid arm' for caning.[49] With four friends, Roald decides to pay back Mrs Pratchett's persistent unfriendliness. As in fairytales and folklore, unexpected reversals upset his plan. Briefly the hero of the hour, who punishes his tormentor by concealing a dead mouse in one of her sweet jars, the Roald of the story is transformed into a contrite murderer when the old woman apparently dies of a heart attack brought on by shock. But Mrs Pratchett is anything but dead, and hell bent on revenge. All five boys are harshly beaten. A wizened Welsh Madame Defarge, 'with a moustache on her upper lip and a mouth as sour as a green gooseberry', Mrs Pratchett watches their suffering gleefully from a seat nearby.[50] Her viciousness and Mr Coombe's sadism confer on Roald an alternative, more sober heroism as suffering martyr. Like Charlie Bucket and protagonists in many of his short stories for adults, the Roald of 'The Great Mouse Plot' is powerless in the face of unfolding events. His power is as storyteller.

'The Great Mouse Plot' is a writer's act of remembrance, edited and recoloured for the marketplace. But Roald did indeed take first steps towards his future calling in Llandaff. Not only was he exposed, quite unprepared, to unfairness; 'at the age of eight,' he remembered, 'I became a mad diary enthusiast'. In a Letts pocket diary with a green leather cover, given to him as a present, he began to record his 'thoughts and hopes and anything important that had happened to me … in the past twenty-four hours'; for his ninth birthday he asked for a larger diary.[51] Afterwards he explained his enjoyment: 'I felt that I was writing not exactly history but anyway the history of my own small life.'[52] In the unpredictable, unaccommodating world of school, without autonomy, intimidated and unsettled, Roald constructed an account of his days. In this narrative he placed himself centrally, acknowledging his smallness nevertheless, a mixture of childish braggadocio and uncertainty that would recur. He determined that his diary must be 'a very secret thing', a means of preserving through private swagger and concealment the view of himself he had previously taken for granted. At home for the holidays he hid it 'in a waterproof tin which I tied with string to the very highest branch of a massive conker tree at the bottom of our garden. I knew it was safe there because none of my sisters had a hope of climbing so high.'[53] From the outset, his picture of the world around him was drawn with bold brushstrokes, including 'things that would have made my mother and sisters stretch their eyes in disbelief had they ever read them'.[54] For the rest of his life he retained a childlike disdain for the ordinary, relishing the sort of detail that stretches the eye in disbelief; his writing frequently included protests against unfairness. His writing room then was a horse chestnut tree in his mother's garden, an eyrie among the topmost branches: in springtime 'a cave of green leaves surrounded by those wonderful white candles'.[55] In this lofty perch, his invisibility thrilled him; in his diary's pages he lived unfettered, beyond observation or criticism, reality invented and perfected and clandestine. In his fiction, fantasy and self-invention repeatedly overlap: to uproarious applause unprepossessing Mr Botibol conducts his imaginary orchestra; secretly, playboy-turned-philanthropist Henry Sugar endows orphanages across the globe. Roald never outgrew this impulse. Late in life he regretted that 'those secret diaries I kept so carefully in my youth' were lost.[56]

Least among Roald's gripes about St Peter's was the lumpy porridge. He brushed aside the seediness of Weston-super-Mare, where boys walked along the concrete slipway at Anchor Head, jumping among the rocks, or, in full school uniform, along the vastness of the sands, or played with clockwork boats in a boating pond and walked to Sunday services at 'All Stinks': All Saints church, Anglo-Catholic and aswirl with incense.[57] Uppermost, the brutality of masters towards boys, 'the fear of the dreaded cane [that] hung over us like the fear of death all the time', one result of a point of view Roald later attributed to The Grand High Witch in *The Witches* that 'children are rrree-volting!'.[58] Caning dominates Roald's recorded memories of St Peter's, as it blackened his memories of his public school, Repton: an abiding cruelty that permanently shaped his views of authority, and accounts for the humiliated teachers of his children's fiction, beginning with Mrs Winter in *The Magic Finger*. He was affronted, appalled, agonized by the shaming and injustice of caning; he chronicled its torments unrelentingly. 'We were caned for doing everything that it was natural for small boys to do,' he wrote in an essay published in 1977, still uncomprehending after half a century.[59] Even after a lifetime, he described St Peter's as 'my dreaded boarding school'.[60]

His first term was a nightmare of homesickness. He drew minuscule comfort from ensuring that, wherever his dormitory, he positioned himself in his bed so that he could look out of the window; he slept facing the sea and, on the 'pale and milky' horizon, Wales and Llandaff and Sofie Magdalene and his sisters. The nastiness of masters and matron astonished him and, taught alongside boys a year older, he struggled with some of his lessons. After his first fortnight, he faked symptoms of appendicitis and won a brief reprieve: three extra days at home. He locked his diary in his tuckbox. Yet the older Roald admitted that *Boy*'s gaudier passages were 'coloured by my natural sense of fantasy' and the reality of much of his time at St Peter's was more varied and less ghoulish.[61] His weekly letters home fizz with enthusiasm – about the natural world, a craze for rollerskating, the progress of his stamp collection. They are full of requests for food, books, his riding breeches, a torch bulb, even conkers, as well as news of his best friend, Douglas Highton, brought up in Turkey and therefore, like Roald, an outsider in St Peter's small, enclosed 'English' world. He chronicles the childhood ailments that rampaged through the eighty or so pupils, and boasts of his sporting prowess, including at conkers. (Even sixty years later he would claim that, 'at the ages of eight, nine and ten', conkers 'brought sunshine to our lives during the dreary autumn term'.)[62] He describes the weather, theatrical performances, the appearance and quirks of masters and a programme of talks on subjects from bird legends to Chinese medicine; bossily he passes on to Sofie Magdalene tidbits of new knowledge, even resorting to diagrams. Alfhild receives a present of £2 from Ludwig Aadnesen, and a guileless Roald is predictably envious. Some letters affirm the bond between mother and son: he tells Sofie Magdalene that he has finished reading a Norse fairytale, *East of the Sun and West of the Moon*; he asks about flowers on his sister Astri's grave, his pets, an orange tree he had planted at home, and Jones the gardener; he mentions letters from Bestepapa and his aunt Astrid. Until around the time of his tenth birthday, he signed his letters with the name Sofie Magdalene used for him: 'Boy' – as reassuring to the writer as to the recipient, a role as much as a name and one that played its part in shaping his letter-writing persona of amiable boisterousness and bravado. Buoyant with slang – 'topphole', 'topping', 'terrific', 'a lucky dog' – his letters gave voice to an image of himself that was as important to Roald as to the mother whom he shielded from his unhappiness, a version of the 'Roald' of his secret diaries, like Sofie Magdalene's edited memories of Harald; ebullient and unstoppable, with interests he later listed as 'New inventions … Eccentricity … Secret information'.[63] The letters' vigour and directness foreshadow his adult writing. Afterwards Roald enjoyed quoting school reports that poured scorn on his achievements in English, his own belated redress to disillusionment. He chose selectively. His half-term report from St Peter's in the summer of 1927, for example, described his performance as 'very fair'.

As much as he could, he read. Books of his own choosing: spy stories and tales of adventure, including standard schoolboy fodder of the time, G. A. Henty and the early novels of C. S. Forester; Marryat's *Mr Midshipman Easy* thrilled him. Like Matilda he rated *The Secret Garden* 'best of all'.[64] He developed a taste for ghost stories. A collection published by Ambrose Bierce thirty years earlier 'profoundly fascinated' him; later, without success, he attempted his own.[65] He read with absorption and viscerally: he would describe a sensation of 'tickles in the tummy' reading poetry.[66] Looking back, he inventoried a child's requirements of fiction: he himself was the child reader he conjured. 'They love being spooked. They love suspense. They love action. They love ghosts. They love the finding of treasure. They love chocolates and toys and money. They love magic.'[67] Thanks to St Peter's, his own tastes expanded. Before his eleventh birthday he had made first sorties into Dickens and Shakespeare and, he told Sofie Magdalene, read *Treasure Island*; he learned five new words a day and 'clear cut … rules of spelling, vocabulary, grammar, reading and writing'.[68] Early in 1927, he wrote his first story, 'The Kumbak II', using a fountain pen given to him by Sofie Magdalene for Christmas: it describes a machine invented by the narrator's 'Uncle Aristotle' that uses radio technology to tune into conversations from the past in 'olden-day language'. By the time he left St Peter's, Roald had enjoyed moments of genuine happiness too, thanks to 'a great and gifted teacher, a scholar and a lover of English Literature': long-haired, yellow-toothed, eccentrically dressed Mrs O'Connor, who visited St Peter's senior boys on Saturday mornings.

Over three years, Mrs O'Connor introduced Roald and his contemporaries to her own version of the story of English, beginning with the Anglo-Saxons and culminating in the Victorian novel. To her an older Roald credited his 'avid and insatiable read[ing] of good writing'.[69] Of course it played its part in his own success. Good writing, he would claim with forthright exaggeration, 'comes automatically from reading'.[70]

II

PLODDING,
ENDLESS TERMS
1930–1934

'An almost limitless black tunnel at the end of which
there glimmered a small bright light.'

ROALD HAD BEEN away from home for two months when, in March 1930, he bought Sofie Magdalene a postcard in the bookshop in the south Derbyshire village of Repton, the site of his public school for the next four years. The postcard reproduced a black-and-white photograph of a meet of the Burton Beagles, attended by numbers of Repton boys. Wearing games kit, Roald himself stands front centre, half turned to face the camera. His expression is hard to read: not quite smiling, not wholly querulous. He is already taller by a head than many of his peers. For his mother he numbered in small neatly inked figures fourteen of the boys with whom he shared his boarding house, The Priory. He identified them on the card's reverse, enabling Sofie Magdalene to put faces to the names in his letters. The long list of boys was a squeeze, preventing Roald from further comment.[1]

In Roald's letters from Repton is the same breeziness that marked his letters from St Peter's. Parcels from home of eggs, cream, dates, plums, cake and occasional Norwegian delicacies provoked enthusiastic thanks; out-of-the-ordinary weather, staff tantrums, sports fixtures, a royal visit, Roald's own recipe for treacle toffee, and a plan to make 'a gigantic fire balloon, to be 18ft high, with a diameter of 12 feet' and capable of lifting 'at least one boy' into the air, provided material for his pen.[2] He worked hard to entertain Sofie Magdalene as once, with folk tales, nursery rhymes and stories of his father, she had entertained him. In a final letter from St Peter's, thirteen-year-old Roald had tripped over himself in pursuit of startling effects: he described the distraction of a boy singing nearby as he wrote, as resembling the noise 'of a fly's kneecap, rattled about in a bilious buttercup, both having kidney trouble and lumbago!'[3] Months later, writing from Repton, he revealed a surer touch in his first pen portrait of 'a short man with a face like a field elderberry': his maths teacher, Major Strickland.[4] Scatological jokes reveal mother and son's shared lack of squeamishness: 'Those figs will keep me going in more sense than one for quite a long time,' Roald quips.[5] With a dramatic flourish he began his letter home the day his study burned down, in the summer of 1931: 'Fire! No one here's talking about anything else.'[6] The flames, he told his mother, had destroyed a new mackintosh, his hockey stick, squash racquet and hair brushes, fused every electric light and left his bed 'brown and nasty'. The teenage Roald appears inconvenienced, chirpily undaunted; the act of letter-writing is itself a pleasure, his tone conversational albeit forceful, and his very forcefulness points to his confidence within what remained his strongest relationship. Nothing spells out the misery that, fifty years later, coloured memories of Repton in his first, unpublished draft of *Boy*, nor does he acknowledge his letters to his mother as an apprenticeship

in storytelling or respite from the systemic boy-on-boy
bullying of The Priory, with its awful burden of fagging –
junior boys acting as servants to senior boys: making toast,
polishing shoes, boots, buttons, cleaning studies, even
warming loo seats. Roald's first intended-for-publication
departed from his letters to Sofie Magdalene: he likened
the ordeal of public school to 'groping through an almost
limitless black tunnel at the end of which there glimmered
a small bright light, and if we ever reached it we would be
eighteen years old'.[7] Overwhelming boredom, he suggested,
contributed to his wretchedness, a succession of 'grey and
melancholy days' through the 'plodding, endless terms';
he dismissed his teachers as 'incredibly dull'.[8] Like others
before and since, he compared school to prison, lamenting
its mercilessness.[9] By contrast, his letters communicated
amusement, enthusiasm, busyness, the pleasures of fleeting
freedoms: empty Sunday afternoons in which he wandered
beyond the Priory gardens, with their scum-thick plunge
pool where boys bathed naked, into surrounding expanses
of Derbyshire countryside, or waking early in the dog days of
the school year to absorb 'a calm that can be experienced only
early on a summer morning, when the sun has just risen'.[10]
Humorous, jolly and bombastic, epistolary Roald shielded
Sofie Magdalene from the view he expressed in a school essay
that, in laughter, lay brief escape from 'gloomy thinking and

melancholy brooding': 'We seek the silly, ridiculous things not because they please us, but because they make us laugh, and laughing does us good and kills depression.'[11]

Excessive punishment and the culture of unrelenting bullying – between masters and boys and, especially, between older and younger boys – were principal causes of Roald's unhappiness. 'I naturally hoped that my long-suffering backside would be given a rest at my new and more adult school, but it was not to be,' he wrote in an essay called 'Lucky Break'. 'The beatings at Repton were more fierce and more frequent than anything I had yet experienced.'[12] Senior boys ruled their juniors 'by fear'.[13] It was an environment dominated by physical abuse and often, in Roald's memories, the cold: icy baths, outdoor lavatories without doors like 'the funny little wooden hut standing in the field some way behind the caravan' that he imagined in *Danny the Champion of the World*, loo seats rimed with frost, sopping wet clothes.[14] From his disaffection emerged stark unhappiness and an all-embracing contempt. The latter endured. In a story called 'Galloping Foxley', written in the early 1950s, Roald's fictional alter ego, William Perkins, conceives an 'impish fancy' to humiliate the senior boy who had once bullied him, encountering him again after an interval of six decades.[15] Roald humiliated his own tormentors in *Boy* – the book's sneering and sadistic prefect,

Carleton, is Roald's worst oppressor, Hugh Middleton. But inaccuracies pepper *Boy*. Mistakenly Roald attributed to one-time Repton headmaster and future Archbishop of Canterbury Geoffrey Fisher a particularly brutal beating inflicted on his best friend, Michael Arnold. In fact, Fisher had left Repton the year before the incident Roald recounted, and Arnold's beating was not, as Roald appears to suggest, a random act of cruelty but punishment for sexual offences involving younger boys, which Repton explained as a mental breakdown and Roald concealed from Sofie Magdalene. Made aware of his mistake, the older Roald declined to revise his text. Even fifty years on he had no interest in exonerating any of the men or boys responsible for a 'pretty crisp' regime he had loathed.[16] His 'lasting impression of horror', he claimed, could not be shaken off.[17] In Roald's version, Middleton/Carleton and Fisher are characters who conform to his preference for 'villains to be terrible'; having skewered them in print, he must have known they would remain so ad aeternum. Gallows humour characterizes doggerel Roald wrote in 1988, responding to a letter about his school days from children in Northern Ireland: 'My teacher loved using the cane. / He thrashed me again and again … I used to wear pants extra thick / To lessen the sting from his stick.'[18] Mostly he remained unamused. Neither as schoolboy nor as adult could he reconcile himself to older boys' gleeful torment of their juniors, and bullies and their comeuppance loom large in his writing. 'Life isn't beautiful and sentimental and clear,' he told a Repton contemporary. 'It's full of foul things and horrid people.'[19] It was a verdict born of disillusionment and protest, and the anger it reveals coloured much of his school experience. In his academic reports, inattention and underperformance are recurring criticisms; among boys of his own age were those who noted a forbidding aloofness about tall teenage Roald. Even at St Peter's, remembered Douglas Highton, 'stupid or unnecessary rules' had provoked Roald's disdain.[20] But esoteric and arcane prescriptions dominated Repton life. Roald's 'twitchy' housemaster, J. S. Jenkyns, known as 'Binks', commented on his stubbornness; other masters correctly identified his subversion. He could be defensive, defiant, arrogant: in the margin of an essay on parliamentary reform, in which his teacher had crossed out discursive sentences, Roald wrote firmly, 'Don't do this on my essays!'[21] He was frequently ill, including with respiratory problems. His lack of focus, obstinacy, simmering revolt and indifferent health seem not to have prompted questions among his teachers. An attentive Sofie Magdalene dispatched the succession of patent medicines that, on each occasion, Roald confirmed restored him to health. In vivid, loving letters, she worked hard to offer tactful reassurance, aware of the extent of his unhappiness at intervals, like the time he suggested her best present for a new godchild would be 'a millstone with instructions as to how it should be hung around the neck while in the bath'.[22] She does not appear to have considered withdrawing him from school.

Repton's spartan regime of games, caning and fagging resembled that of other public schools. The horrors of St Peter's had gone some way to preparing Roald. At his own admission, he suffered less than others. He was not a natural victim – a competent games player (the best squash player in the school and in time captain of both squash and fives, a footballer, cricketer and golfer) and always tall for his age: he was six feet five by his mid-teens. In a class reading of *Romeo and Juliet*, Roald was cast as Romeo on the strength of his voice having broken ahead of his classmates'. Nor were his boyish sensibilities unusually refined: faced with the choice of a ringside seat at any event in history, Roald suggested the murder, in 1801, of the Russian tsar Paul I.[23] He also shared attitudes of the middle-class plutocracy in which he found himself. In a dramatic sketch entitled 'A Conversation with a Pavement Artist', a creative writing task, an enterprising Roald explains to the much older man drawing baskets of fruits in coloured chalks at his feet how to 'do something different, something which will make every man who passes stop and look'. The man is hesitant, lacking Roald's confidence or material certainties; Roald is well-meaning, even entrepreneurial, but overweeningly superior.[24] In other instances, his intentions were less laudable: he excelled at cruel nicknames and learned quickly the 'link between cruelty and laughter' that he would exploit as a writer.[25] Again, his 'natural sense of fantasy' played its part in transforming routine experiences into shilling shocker stuff in his written memories; throughout his time at school he was happy on the playing fields, in the squash and fives courts, in the company of his softly spoken art master, Arthur Norris, who introduced him to the Post-Impressionists – Cezanne and Matisse – and nurtured a nascent interest in art.[26] Reasons for his failure to assimilate himself to Repton lay within Roald himself: fatherless, obdurate and independent, with his Norwegian name, unconventional home life and atypical parental role model in irreverent, plain-speaking Sofie Magdalene. At St Peter's, Douglas Highton remembered, Roald had been considered an outsider, partly on account of his perceived foreignness. At Repton, Roald's separation from his peers was of his own choosing. He rationalized his detachment from the school's ubiquitous hierarchies with catch-all excuses: he disliked rules, the exercise of authority, wielding power.[27] His height, he argued, supplied grounds for exclusion: 'when you're my size you have everything against you. It's very hard to get on with other people.'[28] He discounted his Norwegian heritage: his schooling was the most important factor in his subsequent identification as British. In a history essay on causes of the Indian Mutiny of 1857 Roald is commendably even-handed; on balance, his argument suggests elements of fellow feeling. It was an uprising, he wrote, 'of men who wished to drive out an alien rule, and who had seen the sphere in which they could rise to influence and power steadily and rapidly lessened', like Roald the Apple, accustomed to special treatment at home, cast adrift by Repton's divergent values and standards.[29] Instead he revelled in solitary walks and imaginative flights of fancy that he did not always share with those around him; the adjective he chose for himself was 'dreamy'. Late in his second year, he took up photography, formalizing his standing as onlooker; his preferred subjects were buildings rather than people. Among early successes was a photograph of the school swimming baths, complete with watery reflections. 'You can hardly tell which way up it is,' he wrote proudly to Sofie Magdalene.[30]

Roald absorbed contradictory lessons. In the interests of self-preservation and saving face he learned to suppress instinctive or emotional responses, like the tears that, when he was caned, 'poured down your cheeks in streams and dripped on to the carpet';[31] in his four years at Repton he took further steps in learning how to write. Corporal punishment, he concluded, reduced perpetrator and victim to a primitive state, no longer fully human: 'Wherever we went, we walked carefully, with ears pricked for danger, like wild animals stepping softly through the woods.'[32] By contrast, writing would enable him to articulate his own understanding of what being human meant. As a writer Roald would benefit from a sequence of unofficial mentors: C. S. Forester, Walt Disney, Ernest Hemingway. Before them was John Crommelin-Brown, his English master, known to boys as 'Crummers'. In the decade before Roald's arrival at Repton a county cricketer for Derbyshire, in 1918 Crommelin-Brown had published a volume of war poetry, *Dies Heroica*. The foreword to the slim volume celebrated Crommelin-Brown's ability to capture 'all the eternal childhood of the human heart', a quality that an older Roald would claim for himself and one that proved key to the success of his children's fiction.[33] Crommelin-Brown's assessment of the compromises of communal living surely rang true for Roald at Repton: 'About our beings we create a fence / Built of conventions and hypocrisies … Man makes you false, the gods have built you true; / Think, act and speak the godlike truth in you.'[34] Mostly Crummers' advice to the boys he taught concerned style. 'Don't let P. G. Wodehouse be your master too much,' he wrote on a piece of Roald's creative writing about rich young men amusing themselves by taking up flying.[35] More than once he noted, 'Always use the short word instead of the long one.'[36] Roald heeded both instructions. In time his narrative voice slewed off imitation and he took care to avoid artifice or unnecessary elaboration in his writing; he remembered his English teaching as focused on building sentences that captured precisely what the writer intended, one aspect of his own succinct and pithy manner afterwards.[37] Later, he shared similar advice with younger authors, telling a would-be short story writer in 1980 to 'learn how to write short sentences and how to eschew all those beastly adjectives'; to a government committee considering approaches to teaching English, Roald suggested 'Teach the short sentence. Teach the sparing use of adjectives. Ban the use of "very".'[38] Over time he would repeatedly discuss approaches to writing for children. He stressed the importance of a child-like outlook on the author's part, but he did not acknowledge Repton's role in shaping his fictional world of dark reversals and apparently noxious chance – the combination that, in the 1970s, saw his short stories repackaged as 'Tales of the Unexpected'. Instead, he delighted in flaunting more or less dismissive school reports written by a series of his Repton English teachers with the comment, 'Not much encouragement there to become a writer'.[39] He denied

Repton's part in familiarizing him with what he labelled 'the tricks with words which writers use, which they have to use just as painters have to use tricks with paint'.[40] Unrepentant, he would later conclude, 'I was a very tall boy and most of the masters were very short men and so they didn't like me very much … I was probably arrogant and opinionated.'[41]

It was not in Crummers' company, but alone, or with a single friend like Michael Arnold that Roald found his most reliable escape from school's horrors. Little frequented, Repton's dark room stood at a remove from the core of the school in a converted outbuilding. For Roald it became a second study. It was his Sunday retreat, where his thoughts could be his own and, undisturbed, he could smoke either of the long-stemmed pipes Sofie Magdalene had bought for him in Norway. In the darkroom – quiet, cut off, secret – he found an outlet for the creative urges he had once channelled into his diaries, hiding among the horse chestnut candles in his mother's leafy garden. Among his photographs were composite images: montages of snapshots of his friends and of Repton landmarks assembled to create a reordering of his Repton world. Given the complexities of photography in the 1920s, he also found there opportunities for arcane ingenuity of a sort that would always appeal to him: among the glass plate negatives and acrid chemicals he resembled Willy Wonka in his 'marvellous workshop full of wheels and wires and buckets of glue and balls of string and pots full of thick hot foaming stuff that gives off smoke in many colours'.[42] That the business of photography was time-consuming and deterred the uninitiated were among its recommendations for Roald. Of the photographs he developed there, a clutch won public prizes, including from the Royal Photographic Society. *Contra Boy*, one picture showed a smiling Geoffrey Fisher.

Like his diary keeping at St Peter's, photography enabled Roald to capture and fix a particular view of the world around him. Reassurance, however, was not uppermost among his needs. Repton's cat's cradle of rules and grey unhappiness stoked an appetite for adventure: the narrative posturing of Roald's letters points to a desire to flex his muscles, escape, expand. Firmly he rejected Sofie Magdalene's suggestion of Oxford or Cambridge: he had no intention of prolonging his experience of institutionalized learning. With the confidence he had expressed in a school essay – 'go to some firms and tell them you are an expert … They would jump at [you]' – he wrote letters to a handful of companies likely to send him 'to wonderful faraway places like Africa or China'.[43] To his own surprise and the disgruntled astonishment of his housemaster, and partly through the intervention of a family friend, he received an offer of employment from the Shell Company (Eastern Staff) – later, he attributed his success to his status as school heavyweight boxing champion, proof of his physical fitness.[44] And thanks to the acquisition in 1932 of a 500cc Ariel motorcycle, in his final years at school he realized the version of himself that, at seventeen, he valued highest: daring, rule-breaking, speedy and, above all, free. Disguised by helmet, goggles, raincoat and waders, he roared through Repton, lord of the narrow lanes, inwardly thumbing his nose at dim brick classroom buildings and the prefects and masters he passed. His swagger was insolent, after years of reluctant compliance. By arrangement he kept the bike in a barn some distance away, another secret, at one with the country folk whose casual dishonesties would pepper his stories: Claud switching greyhounds in 'Mr Feasey'; Ford keen to swindle Gordon Butcher out of his reward in 'The Mildenhall Treasure'. The element of secrecy added to Roald's enjoyment. 'There are no secrets unless you keep them to yourself,' he reflected afterwards.[45] Time would show he had a talent for secrets. School Certificate examinations in English, French, History, Scripture Knowledge and Elementary Maths signalled the end of Roald's formal schooling. Though adequate, his results would not have earned him the place at Oxford or Cambridge Sofie Magdalene dreamed of, even had he wanted it. His final school report commended 'a real artistic sense' that Roald may not have suspected staff glimpsed in him.[46] A disappointed Sofie Magdalene paid an astrologer for a reading of his horoscope. Time would confirm its accuracy.

For Roald, Repton's sole advantage over other public schools was an arrangement with chocolate-makers Cadbury's. 'Once a term each boy was given free of charge a small brown box,' he wrote in 1975.

> Inside the box there were eight chocolate bars, a present from Cadbury's. Seven of the bars were new inventions not on the market. The eighth was one that even in those days, we all knew well, the glorious Dairy Milk Flake. And in return for this gift we were required to taste and give our expert opinions on each new invention, giving it points from 0 to 10 and making carefully considered comments. We also marked the eighth bar, which then served as a control.'[47]

This unexpected boon encouraged Roald's taste for high-street chocolate. It inspired dreams of working for Cadbury's, inventing all manner of new and delicious chocolate treats: 'Suddenly I would shout "I've got it!" and I would dash out of the room with my new discovery straight into the office of Mr Cadbury himself.'[48] In time, it inspired one of the best-loved and biggest-selling of his novels for children, *Charlie and the Chocolate Factory*, a Cinderella story of dreams coming true, just deserts for bullies and childhood anxieties allayed by a magical deus ex machina in the form of resourceful, rule-breaking mythomane, Willy Wonka.

III

FIT AND TOUGH

1934–1940

'Where no one (so they say) has ever been before.'

ACONVERSATION ABOUT LONDON restaurants in the summer of 1934, recorded by Roald in his diary, revealed lifelong preoccupations. 'It was the Cheshire Cheese, Simpsons, Gattis – Roast Beef, Irish stews, Toad in the Hole, Honeycomb and Cream … Then the subject would suddenly turn to literature and music.'[1] Roald was seventeen. With the passage of time he might have added to this tally of food, music and books, golf, girls and greyhound racing. He was mistrustful of authority, irreverent and self-possessed, with a strong feeling for family. Leaving school behind him, his chief taste was for excitement.

The aim of the third expedition of the Public Schools Exploring Society, its organizer explained, was 'to take British schoolboys into uninhabited wilds, to teach them to fend for themselves, to widen their outlook and, above all, to foster the spirit of adventure.'[2] To Sofie Magdalene, Roald had described it as four weeks 'in the wilds of Newfoundland! which hasn't been mapped before so a bit of surveying would be done for the Government too.'[3] Surgeon Commander George Murray Levick, known as 'the Admiral', a veteran of Scott's doomed Antarctic expedition two decades earlier, had previously led parties of schoolboys to Finland and Lapland. At a cost of £35, Roald joined him, his helpers and a group of forty-seven boys, among them a Repton friend called Jimmy Horrocks, with whom he later went climbing in Snowdonia, and an eager schoolboy ornithologist, K. B. Rooke, on a march 'where no one (so they say) has ever been before', a hundred miles inland across Canada's north-eastern province.[4] For the first time, Roald was absent from the family party on Tjome. He described his temporary replacement family as 'very nice ... with the exception of an odd tough here & there'.[5]

The prospect of privations that would shortly become all but overwhelming seems hardly to have registered at the outset: perhaps Roald's expectations were shaped by memories of school field days, like a day on Cannock Chase in Staffordshire in November 1932, 'a marvellous place: thousands of acres of heather & bracken on a deeply undulating plain'.[6] His ship sailed from Liverpool; on the voyage out, Roald enjoyed a flirtation with an actress from the Liverpool Repertory Company called Ruth Lodge, two years his senior. Proudly he reported his success to his mother, noting the envy of his forty-seven fellow teenage explorers; in the same letter, a distant iceberg engages quite as much of his attention. Like Cannock Chase, Newfoundland offered unbroken acres of low-level vegetation, thick with insects, frequently sodden with rain: it was an intractable setting for lengthy marches and nights spent five boys to each small tent, often cold, often wet, 'too tired to talk much when we turned in at about 8.30'.[7] Roald's heavy backpack included his tobacco and two pipes, a mouth organ, his fishing rod, camera and lead-cased rolls of film, as well as his allocation of the party's food rations. He packed no shaving equipment and promptly lost his toothbrush. He described his improvised replacement, made from a nailbrush, as 'moderately efficient – for a horse it would have been excellent'.[8]

It ought not to surprise us that his feelings for Murray Levick swiftly declined from admiration to disillusionment and, via resentment, to active dislike. The attitude of the self-styled 'Admiral' towards his charges – inflexible, inconsiderate, braggart – too closely replicated master-and-boy relationships at St Peter's and Repton; Roald blamed Murray Levick for the party's dwindling morale and unnecessary discomforts. Twelve days before the expedition ended, Roald ripped a six-inch-long hole in one of his boots; he managed a makeshift but uncomfortable repair, and the boot remained 'a happy home for any bog water that doesn't know where to go'.[9] Among the party, persistent hunger produced 'a slightly mutinous air' that anti-authoritarian Roald did not regret; he was among the small group who, prompted by what he described as misery beyond anything 'any of us have ever felt', challenged Murray Levick's plans.[10] He noted the cruelty of trapping animals in snares, a predator–prey relationship of overwhelming inequalities – his response a foreshadowing of feelings that inspired the comeuppance of Farmers Boggis, Bunce and Bean in *Fantastic Mr Fox* and the contempt of Danny's father for fat cat Victor Hazell in *Danny the Champion of the World*. Of rabbits caught in the traps he had set, Roald commented that it '[wasn't] exactly humane, & we wouldn't have done it if we hadn't been pretty hard put to it for food'.[11] 'I've always felt very strongly about injustices and cruelty,' he told an interviewer fifty years later.[12] Revealingly, he described 'justifiable anger' as a 'natural emotion' in the face of injustice. Certainly it was the reaction that came naturally to Roald – both in Newfoundland and ever after.

Once it was over, he seems not to have given the expedition much thought – unlike K. B. Rooke, who, from notes in his diary, wrote articles for specialist magazine *British Birds*: 'Birds seen in the North Atlantic, August and September, 1934' and 'Observations on the Birds of Newfoundland during the 1934 expedition of the Public Schools Exploring Society'. For Roald the trip had served its purpose; he set aside his Newfoundland diary in a notebook that remained mostly empty. 'It *was* a genuine adventure,' he concluded. 'I returned home hard and fit and ready for anything.'[13]

'Anything' took the form of four years' training with Shell, then the Asiatic Petroleum Company: office work in the company's headquarters in the City of London and weeks of

practical salesmanship, including in rural Somerset. Roald's
account, written at a remove of time, reveals his tendency
to reformat experience to conform to patterns of childhood
narratives and something, too, of his turkeycock swagger:
from his memories of selling kerosene in West Country
villages he emerges as the hero of a rustic fairytale. At the
roar of his car engine, 'the old girls and the young maidens'
appeared at their cottage doors holding out jugs and buckets
for young Roald to fill, an obvious metaphor. Office life
itself provoked a more ambivalent response. The bowler hat
and silk umbrella of the London businessman-commuter
reinforced a sense of his new maturity; he was aware of an
element of play acting and, perhaps, in this conventional
interlude, of treading water. Thoughts of writing were at best
embryonic. 'I'm very much against young people thinking
they want to be writers … Writing is a thing you sort of
flow into,' he reflected in 1979, suggesting that this had
been his own experience, the Shell years marked instead
by a young man's delight in the world around him, which
was mostly true.[14] Beyond a characteristically ebullient
spoof contributed to *The Shell Magazine* in 1937, Roald's
encounters with writing in his twenties were as a reader.
He would remember his six-times-a-week train journey
into London for its opportunities for reading new fiction:
novels by Hemingway, Damon Runyon and, especially,

Graham Greene – stories he would continue to enjoy, written in a more or less 'masculine' idiom that found its echo the following decade in the bold crossfire of Roald's own first fictions; he read Karen Blixen's *Seven Gothic Tales* and, on publication in 1937, *Out of Africa*. On his desk in Shell headquarters in St Helen's Court he saved the silver paper wrappers of the chocolate bars he ate every day after lunch, wrapping them one around the next. Eventually something the size of a tennis ball, they point to an element of boredom alongside his enthusiasm for Flakes, Crunchie bars and Rowntree's Chocolate Crisps (later renamed Kit Kats). Energy and stubborn independence did not make Roald a natural office trainee. 'If he was told to do things – bah! he wasn't interested,' remembered a fellow trainee.[15] His description of himself then as 'a conventional young lad from the suburbs' was, as he knew, as misleading as his homogenizing uniform of bowler hat and umbrella, and his thoughts remained focused on the overseas posting that would signal the end of his probationary period: 'no furled umbrellas, no bowler hats, no sombre grey suits and … never once … a train or a bus'.[16]

For the first time since the age of nine, Roald lived at home. Retrospectively it appeared an easygoing chapter, free from the tragedies that chequered his experiences as husband and father, even if he understood, unspoken, the extent of his mother's disappointment in this ordinary-seeming turn in his affairs. First hierarchies fell back into place. Roald was once again 'the Apple' of a mostly admiring sorority of Alfhild, Else, Asta and, of course, Sofie Magdalene. An American friend would refer to him living among 'a thousand sisters' in 'a suffocating atmosphere of adoration'.[17]

At the time of the Dahls' move an overgrown village in Kent, subsequently absorbed by Greater London, Bexley was less than 20 miles from St Pancras Station, with its train links to Roedean, where, in 1927, Alfhild had already begun school, and Euston, where, from 1930, Roald took the train to Repton. A reminder to us of the Dahls' comfortable circumstances, Oakwood – like Cumberland Lodge – stood in spacious gardens; there was a tennis court, a large conservatory, extensive cellars. Of Harald Dahl's six surviving children, only Ellen had married by the time Roald returned from Newfoundland in the autumn of 1934. Louis, Alfhild, Else and Asta continued to make their home with Sofie Magdalene. Temporarily others joined this noisy ménage, including a friend Roald had made in Canada, Dennis Pearl. Louis' painting studio occupied the house's top floor; Roald had a fully equipped dark room; in Sofie Magdalene's drawing room stood the Bechstein piano on which Alfhild and Else played duets by Beethoven, Roald's favourite composer. Happy in one another's company, the unconventional household moved through the dark decade of the 1930s with few evident concerns about approaching danger. Harald's fortune and attentive domestic staff continued for the time being to safeguard their comfort, though by the decade's end the dwindling value of Aadnesen & Dahl shares would significantly reduce Sofie Magdalene's income – a possible explanation for the advertisements she placed in the *Western Mail* over five days in December 1937, for a houseparlourmaid and kitchenmaid. Beyond satisfactory references, she stipulated only that applicants 'must know some cooking', perhaps an attempt to avoid the expense of a new cook.[18] Roald's single living expense consisted of his train fares. His weekends were full of golf, Sibelius on his gramophone, greyhound racing at nearby Catford Stadium, and a sequence of more or less furtive romantic and sexual entanglements, including with older married women, that give the lie to his version of himself as 'a bundle of youthful self-consciousness'.[19]

In the autumn of 1938, Roald's response to his posting to East Africa was one of delight. Karen Blixen's account of her Kenyan farm and a taste for the exotic that would never leave him coloured his reaction; he was undeterred by fears of the prescriptions of British colonial life, the narrowness of outlook and rigid shibboleths of a society as hermetic as any boarding school community. His destination was Dar es Salaam, capital of the British protectorate of Tanganyika (modern-day Tanzania). The journey by sea took a fortnight; as Roald and Sofie Magdalene both understood, there would be no return visits to break up Roald's three-year absence. Sofie Magdalene was stoical in the face of this latest separation: mother and son acknowledged, but did not dwell upon, the likelihood of the outbreak of war in Roald's absence. His response to school had accustomed Roald to isolation: his appointment to a team of only three, in an operation launched by Shell as recently as 1936, did not trouble him, nor the mundanity of selling lubricating and fuel oil to farmers scattered across a country four times the size of Britain. 'Not a great deal of intelligence or imagination was required,' he admitted in old age, 'but by gum you needed to be fit and tough.'[20] It was Newfoundland all over again.

Over time, Roald's view of the year he spent in East Africa would change. Cheap domestic help invested colonial life with a luxurious dimension Roald came to regard as wrong. In 1938, accustomed to the solid comforts of his mother's rambling, well-staffed house in Bexley, and conditioned by an imperial mindset that elevated Britishness to a virtue, Roald partly acquiesced in a way of life grounded in racial inequalities. In the Dar es Salaam Club, he lived like 'a ridiculous young pukka-sahib' and the lightness of his workload left hours for 'golf or tennis or squash or swimming or sailing' and evening drinks, called 'sundowners', in some quantity;[21] his salary disappeared in the rituals and trappings of empire: his bar bills, 'club entrance fees, new white suits, white shirt and goodness knows what else – expensive topees and mosquito boots'.[22] As much as Repton, Tanganyika's British community valued conformity. Roald was predictably irritated. Elderly empire hands goaded him to exhibitionism, brusquerie, outspokenness – drinks party pranks like a chamber pot stolen from a bedroom and paraded on his head. Roald's letters to Sofie Magdalene reassured her of nothing untoward in his drinking, while chronicling with bravado a punishing intake, the scrapes and hangovers and fleeting lapses of memory this involved. In January 1939, with colleagues George Rybot and Panny Williamson, he moved into a house built for its employees by Shell. He described his pride in his household management: 'I'm the housekeeper. Every morning at breakfast I hold my court,' including ordering meals – pigeon casserole, sheep's brains in spinach, 'crabs ad infinitum' or turbot recipes sent from home, adapted to suit native koli-koli; one photograph shows him in shorts and a solar topee collecting fallen coconuts under palm trees.[23] A staff of five, including a gardener, kept house and occupants in apple-pie order; in addition to Roald, Rybot and Williamson were

a dog called Samka and two Persian cats, Oscar and Mrs
Taubsypuss. The house itself stood metres from the sea.
Postcard-perfect views encompassed a towering baobab
tree and, beyond it, 'the coastline stretching away on both
sides as far as you can see'.[24] Here, on the very margins of
the Indian Ocean, where land and sea met, Roald briefly
enjoyed another neverland, like the unpeopled beaches
and scattered villages of the Oslo-fjord and Tjome.[25] On
the shallow steps of the house's broad verandah, in short-
sleeved shirts in place of the customary evening dress, the
three men entertained members of the British community
to sundowners and Roald's limited selection of gramophone
records, including Beethoven's Third and Fifth Symphonies.
Months later, Roald moved again, this time to a house on
his own. Only a pair of lizards, whom he named Hitler
and Mussolini, and the inevitable native servants intruded
on a set-up as cheerfully isolated as the dark room at
Repton. He might have been expected to have filled empty
evenings with reading: in his letters to Sofie Magdalene,
like Uncle Aristotle in his 'wireless room' in the story
Roald wrote when he was ten, music and the radio feature
more prominently; he was learning, he remembered
afterwards, to speak Swahili and drink whisky.[26] Roald's
life would include few such interludes of seclusion. More
often his homes were full of women: Sofie Magdalene

and his sisters; his wives, daughters, stepdaughters and grandchildren.

Far away were the familiar landmarks of the commuter belt. Often bored, often physically uncomfortable, Roald nevertheless rejoiced in Tanganyika's exoticism: 'Giraffe [stood] unafraid right beside the road nibbling the tops of the trees'; there were elephants, hippopotamus, zebra and antelopes.[27] Even the climate was otherworldly: unendurably hot, Roald claimed, by eight-thirty in the morning, made bearable by early-evening cold baths and dinner eaten in his dressing gown. Presents from Sofie Magdalene of a Stilton cheese and foie gras, and books in Norwegian sent by his grandparents, offered reminders of his former life and Harald's wealth. Sofie Magdalene's dispatch of a recently published guide to curing constipation and obesity recalled mother and son's school correspondence over patent medicines and Roald's preoccupation with his health.

None of Roald's children's stories and only a fraction of his other writings engage directly with East African subjects. Inevitably, his African posting – stopped short by the advent of war – played its part in his development as a writer. A tyro colonialist, his perceptions of Africa and African lives were shaped by then current fictions: narratives of empire, race, plunder, adventure. Still excited by eye-stretching details, Roald could not react neutrally to an environment that spawned the stories he included in his second volume of autobiography, *Going Solo* – a green mamba snake several metres in length that silently killed a British family's Airedale terrier as it sheltered from the sun beneath a table, or the elderly lion that made away with the wife of a native cook only to drop her from its jaws entirely unharmed after she pretended to be dead – even if there is little evidence that Roald himself witnessed either spectacle. The effect of the heat on his countrymen prompted descriptions recognizable to readers of his children's books: a fat man sweating, 'flowing over his chair like a hot jellyfish – and he's steaming too. He may melt.'[28] In Africa, the survival of inherited patterns of behaviour and belief, like the warrior instincts of Roald's personal servant Mdisho, a Mwanumwezi tribesman, and an age-old relationship between man and his surrounds, including potentially deadly wildlife, added up, in Roald's eyes, to a region simultaneously untouched and magical; his contempt for British colonialists in a story called 'Poison' targets their racism and, thousands of miles from home, their adherence to a mindset impervious to the marvels close at hand. 'To me it was all wonderful, beautiful and exciting,' Roald wrote of Dar es Salaam and its palm-tree-lined harbour on the ocean.[29] Much in his African life, with its unvarying 'string of sundowners' and unforgiving climate, was anything but, but Roald's wonder at Tanganyika's differentness was sincere. Already ingrained was the belief he would express at the end of his life that 'those who don't believe in magic will never find it'.[30]

Home, by contrast, served as his chief source of disquiet. Roald accepted as his due his pivotal role in Dahl family life; long distance, he felt keenly his responsibility towards his mother and sisters. His certainty of the imminence of war focused on a steady – and accurate – conviction that Bexley would find itself on German bombers' flight paths. Firmly he encouraged Sofie Magdalene to move, preferably to the safety of the Welsh coast. Equally firmly, she resisted. Time, of course, proved Roald right. 'I'm very glad to see that you are all ready to shoot off to Tenby,' he wrote on 9 April 1939.[31] It did not happen. Only a raid of the sort Roald had feared – in early September, a clutch of bombs dropped in Oakwood's garden that blew out windows, brought down ceilings and, shortly afterwards, led to official requisitioning – forced Sofie Magdalene, her daughters and their gaggle of dogs from the large, comfortable house, with its paintings by Laura Knight and Frank Brangwyn and cellar stocked with champagne and good brandy. They moved to neighbouring Buckinghamshire, where Alfhild and her husband had settled after their marriage the previous year. The county would remain their home and, in time, Roald's too, still convincingly rural despite its proximity to London, its remoteness expressed for Roald in 'the broad soft accent of the Buckinghamshire countryside' that survived within tight-knit village communities.[32]

Roald's own war began later. For two months following the outbreak of hostilities, he and his Shell colleagues were prevented from leaving Tanganyika; the familiar round of schoolboy-style snake hunts and boozy parties continued. In this uneasy limbo, Roald wrote to Sofie Magdalene of plans to go to Kenya 'if I get the chance', to train as a pilot.[33] His chance came in the second week of November. Like the young man in 'An African Story', 'he made his way over the country to Nairobi, and he reported to the RAF and asked that they make him a pilot'.[34] He passed his medical, he boasted, 'with flying colours'. One of sixteen new trainee pilots, he reported to RAF headquarters outside the Kenyan capital at the end of the month.

Mythomania played its part in Roald's life, sometimes casual, at other times more determined: he took for granted aspects of heroism in his own make-up. The posturing of his early letter-writing – full of swank, shielding Sofie Magdalene (and himself) from the full brunt of his schoolboy unhappiness – and his formative exposure to Norse folklore, with its cast of giants and trolls, shaped a predisposition that his wartime experiences confirmed. In a television documentary after his death, his widow, Liccy, pointed to a tendency to dramatize his military exploits. Self-dramatization was always an aspect of his self-identity and frequently harmless. Roald valued the unusual, those improbable details he had confided to his first diaries during his time at St Peter's, the stories of black and green mambas he preserved in *Going Solo*; in equal measure he valued vividness and intensity of feeling. Between 1939 and 1941, his experiences as a fighter pilot offered intensities of fear, pain, excitement, bravery and, in his own record, initiative that, unsurprisingly, coloured his self-perception ever after; he came close – very close indeed – to death. Memories of this sort, he claimed plausibly, did not recede. He described his experiences as a fighter pilot as 'so vivid and so violent that they remain etched on the memory like something that happened last month'.[35] Of course they shaped his personal mythology.

His training occupied most of the war's first year. Two months in Nairobi were followed by transfer to 'the worst climate in the world', Habbaniya in Iraq. Roald remembered Habbaniya as 'a boiling desert on the banks of the muddy Euphrates river'; for six months he lived in a 'dirty little tent, washing and shaving every day in a mugful of one's own spat-out tooth water, all the time picking flies out of one's tea and out of one's food ... having very little except sand

sand sand'; a sortie to the ancient city of Babylon offered brief respite.³⁶ For all Roald's antipathy to camp life, the interlude inspired a fascination with the region that lasted: the hero of his final short story for adults, Robert Sandy, longs to share his creator's experiences and to visit 'some of the grand remote regions of Asia Minor and also the now below-ground village of Babylon in Iraq and … the Arch of Ctesiphon and the Sphinx at Memphis'.³⁷

Cut short by the accident that changed his life's trajectory, Roald's career in the air would be markedly briefer than his training period and, for Roald, more romantic. It accounted for a love of flying and relish of his own prowess that never left him; it inspired the ten stories published in 1946 as *Over to You* (subtitled '10 stories of flyers and flying') and passages in *James and the Giant Peach* and *Charlie and the Great Glass Elevator*. Billy, the hero of *The Minpins*, is exhilarated by night-time flights on the back of a swan, 'up in the air … the air swishing past his face … in a magical world of silence, swooping and gliding over the dark world below where all the earthly people were fast asleep in their beds' – liberated and intoxicated by freedom and speed, like the teenage Roald racing through Repton's narrow streets on his motorbike, or Roald the fighter pilot alive to the wonder of aircraft, 'like a man on a magic carpet, sitting there alone in this little glass-topped cockpit'.³⁸

But Roald's experiences as a pilot in wartime were predictably less serene than Billy's nocturnal flits. From the outset he was determined to excel, 'orderly and precise' in his approach, as he describes one of his fictional pilots.[39] More than most airmen, he felt for himself the air swishing past his face. At six feet five and a half inches, he was too tall for the windshields of the open-cockpit biplanes the RAF had introduced as training planes earlier in the decade. Over his nose and mouth – exposed to the full force of onrushing air – he tied a cloth to prevent himself from choking. His lessons in the tiny Tiger Moth plane accounted for fewer than eight supervised hours before he began flying solo. His mastery was easy and, he thought, assured, and as he flew he watched the plains below him, their scattering of wildlife, again the camera-toting schoolboy who had observed his surrounds from behind the shield of the lens. Undoubtedly, Roald found flying beautiful. War, he would discover, was not.

The accident that almost ended his pilot's career before it began took the form of a bungled forced landing in the Egyptian desert. In a fictional reworking of these events, Roald would suggest he remembered:

> the dipping of the nose of the aircraft and I remember
> looking down the nose of the machine at the ground and
> seeing a little clump of camel-thorn, and the camel-thorn

and the sand and the rocks leaped out of the ground and came to me ... Then there was a small gap of not remembering. It might have been one second or it might have been thirty.[40]

He had set off from Fouka, in northern Egypt, in September 1940. With him he carried confidential instructions concerning the whereabouts of 80 Squadron, which he was to join as part of an offensive targeting Italian forces on the move from eastern Libya. It was late in the day when Roald embarked on the final flight of his long journey. Within an hour, darkness would swallow up a blinding desert sunset, the sky 'mysterious, menacing, overwhelming' as he pictured it later.[41] Roald had received no training at all in flying the old-fashioned Gloster Gladiator plane; his directions from the commanding officer at Fouka were misleadingly casual, possibly even inaccurate. It was not that he panicked. Above the featureless sands he was swiftly adrift and, as the light thickened and his fuel gauge dipped, he became convinced he could not regain his course. To hazard a forced landing was simply to follow his training. He acted quickly – but luck was against him. At some speed the plane's undercarriage struck a boulder. It set in motion a rapid sequence that destroyed the aircraft and came close to killing Roald. With a frightful lurch, the plane's nose dived, crumpled, concertinaed; it hurled Roald forward. He hit the metal reflector-sight so hard that his nose was forced backwards through his face. His skull fractured, his skin was sticky with blood, he could no longer feel his teeth. He was blinded and frighteningly hot, in danger of being engulfed by the flames that would soon consume the devastated Gladiator. Time halted, hung. For an interval Roald was torn between surrender and resistance, the swift inevitability of death or, more painfully, extracting himself from the twisted cockpit. In his burning overalls he crawled from the wreckage towards the sand. Into the desert silence exploded the plane's machine guns, activated by the heat, showering their deadly cargo: percussive, Roald remembered, in their aimless assault on sand and stones. 'I did not worry about them; I merely heard them,' he wrote in a story called 'A Piece of Cake'.[42] None of the bullets hit him. Instead, burned, bloodied and paralysed by pain, he was eventually overtaken by sleep.

A fellow pilot, Douglas McDonald, watched over him throughout the night that, decades later, Roald explained to his daughter Ophelia was the worst moment of his life; he lay beside Roald in an effort to keep him warm. Both men had left Fouka at the same time. Witnessing Roald's distress, McDonald had landed his plane nearby. In early accounts Roald acknowledged this night-long vigil in the black cold of the desert. Later, his storytelling excluded the other man. The version of his wartime crash as a solo experience that Roald polished into anecdote was not intended to downgrade McDonald but to exonerate himself, a denial of vulnerability that, while it lasted, was all too real. In Roald's account of events, his own role is that of daring fighter ace, brought down by enemy fire, alone bar his resolve: it is one of the 'moments of brilliance and glory' that, in *Boy*, he claimed everyone experiences.[43] In one form or another, single-handed endeavour, coloured by brilliance or even glory, was always his picture of himself.

For the better part of a month he remained unseeing, exhausted, in painful, crippling darkness. RAF authorities attributed his crash to inexperience.

IV

STALKY
1940–1943

'Very colourful and rather unusual scenes.'

As a well-known children's writer in the 1980s, Roald reimagined a collection of fairytales in verse. 'I guess you think you know this story. You don't,' he teased readers at the beginning of his 'revolting' Cinderella.[1]

The desire to confound expectation, linked to dogmatic, uninhibited, sometimes taunting, sometimes teasing inclinations, was characteristic: he felt the same of readers' assumptions about himself. For the Roald who became the world's most commercially successful children's author – a grandfatherly figure of stooping height and long cardigans, 'old and bent and crinkly faced', as he imagined himself – near-fatal heroism was a key ingredient in his own unexpected life story.[2]

He cherished his brush with death. Sofie Magdalene, he claimed, taught all her children 'always [to] treat dangerous situations as great adventures', and Roald reimagined the most dangerous moment of his life accordingly.[3] On the table in his writing hut in the garden of Gipsy House in years to come, Roald's miscellany of Roaldiana included a stone fragment of cuneiform script he had found on his trip to Babylon during pilot training in Iraq; above his chair he fixed a card with a picture of a Gloster Gladiator given to him by his second wife Liccy. Like other objects in his writing hut, visible reminders of his pilot training and his plane crash constituted a segment in Roald's personal jigsaw puzzle. He had destroyed his plane and almost destroyed himself, but events in the Libyan desert in the autumn of 1940, which he summarized as 'a monumental bump' and 'the great bash' on the head, proved the principal turning point in his life.[4] A year later, his active service ended. Then a chance encounter in a different continent encouraged him to record his experiences. Unplanned and mostly unpremeditated, he discovered he had become a writer, the very outcome predicted for him the previous decade by the astrologer consulted by Sofie Magdalene: his flying accident supplied his earliest material. Roald admitted of this career switch, at the end of his life, that 'there was quite a bit of good fortune involved'.[5] Mostly he preferred to attribute it to possible physiological changes in the wake of his wartime injuries. He found another explanation in astrology, writing that Virgoans, of whom he was one, 'often develop surprising artistic qualities when they get older'.[6] Both interpretations invested his writer's calling with an otherworldly alchemy that appealed to competitive instincts in Roald.

In the first instance were slow weeks of recovery in the Anglo-Swiss Hospital in Alexandria. Doctors doubted Roald's ability to recover: he was sightless and all but immobile. If he shared their misgivings, he held out nevertheless for the possibility, however slight, of a return to active service, characteristic stubbornness on the part of a man disinclined to acknowledge frailty. To his sister Asta he dictated a telegram: 'Only concussion broken nose. Absolutely okay soon.'[7] In fact he was plagued by loss of memory, extreme tiredness and fearsome headaches that would persist. A plastic surgeon rebuilt his nose, taking as his model, Roald claimed, film star Rudolph Valentino. Roald thanked the nurses who looked after him with presents of gold watches. Later stages of his convalescence had a sybaritic aspect. In the home of wealthy British expats Teddy and Dorothy Peel, Roald encountered for the first time the comforts of the rich that would always attract him (even when the rich themselves goaded him to contempt).

He was declared fit to return to service in February 1941. As he wrote to Else, uppermost among his thoughts was his desire to rejoin his squadron. This happened two months later, after two weeks training flying a Mark I Hurricane. His destination then was Greece, invaded by Germany on 6 April. With no experience of combat, Roald would take his place among pilots from 80 and 33 Squadrons engaged in ferocious conflict over Athens and its harbour at Piraeus, a 'tiny band of Hurricane pilots ... taking on an overwhelming force of the Luftwaffe who were pushing into Greece preparatory to taking Crete,' as his widow described events in a letter to *The Times* on the fiftieth anniversary in 1991.[8] Setting off from Fouka the previous autumn, Roald may have had a sense of invulnerability. Months later, his anticipation was febrile. His recovery, he knew, was incomplete and his training in flying Hurricanes no more than rudimentary; he continued to suffer debilitating headaches.

Roald described what happened in Greece to Sofie Magdalene the following month. Passages in his letters were matter of fact, sparsely descriptive. At times a mixture of understatement and exaggeration betrayed his unsettlement in the aftermath of long, frenetic, tense, angry, excited, uncertain days in the air that, at least once, left him so physically shaken he was unable to light his cigarette. 'It wasn't much fun taking on half the German Air Force with literally a handful of fighters,' he told his mother.[9] On 16 April, he shot down his first enemy plane. He did the same two days later. He killed again in the main engagement on 20 April. An unequal contest in which British planes were significantly outnumbered, the Battle of Athens claimed the lives of four of the fifteen RAF pilots who took to the sky. In *Going Solo*, Roald's account of this 'long-lasting dog fight' has a breathless excitability; he would remember it as 'in a way the most exhilarating time I have ever had in my life'.[10] But he would also conclude that the sense of detachment he had developed to shield him at St Peter's and Repton hardened in the wake of battle, a quality that would play its part in his relationships. Days later, with other survivors, Roald was flown back to Egypt. He returned to the Peels in Alexandria. Within less than a month, he had rejoined remnants of 80 Squadron in Haifa, in British Palestine. On this occasion, Vichy French were the target. Roald shot down at least two French planes, but he was struggling against a different enemy. Searing headaches caused temporary blackouts flying; doctors declared him unfit for action. He could not protest, despite overwhelming disappointment. Much later, he would suggest that his forced exit from the arena of war brought to an end youthful combativeness.[11] In fact, in Libya, Greece and Palestine, he had absorbed unwelcome lessons: his own undoubted bravery and skilfulness as a pilot, partnered with flashes of physical impuissance. The disappointment of this antithesis – heroism versus pregnability – would further harden his detachment. His later statement that 'I don't think one ever gets over anything … You have just got to go on', ostensibly about family tragedy, also reflected his response to his enforced grounding.[12]

A neighbour in the village of Grendon Underwood described the home to which Roald returned as 'a small old cottage with few facilities'.[13] Thatched, half-timbered and white-painted, half-hidden behind thick hedges, Sofie

Magdalene's first Buckinghamshire cottage had little in common with Oakwood or Cumberland Lodge bar its large garden, and even less that recalled the landscape of citrus groves and fig trees on the margins of the Mediterranean that Roald had left behind. Nor, following the marriages of Alfhild, Else and Louis, was the cottage a nexus for Dahl siblings and half-siblings as Roald remembered. In his description of his homecoming in *Going Solo*, the only reunion Roald mentions is with Sofie Magdalene, throwing himself into her arms as he stepped from the bus that had brought him on the last stage of his journey. She alone was there to greet him. 'I flew down the steps of the bus into the arms of the waiting mother,' Roald wrote, and in his description of the longed-for moment 'my mother' has become 'the mother'.[14] His relationship with Sofie Magdalene remained his strongest emotional connection: after three years' absence, she had become the archetype of every maternal instinct he craved. Her vigil at the garden gate suggests that Roald was still her 'Apple', his own use of the definite article that his chiefest need was for the reassurance that only his mother could provide. In 'Only This', the story in which he imagined a mother's feelings for her pilot son, the son in question is an only child, his mother's single focus. Her thoughts of him fill her remote cottage – like Sofie Magdalene's, a honeycomb of small rooms.

Yet home life proved as changed as every other aspect of wartime existence. With its noisy wooden staircase and low ceilings, Grendon Cottage seemed to shrink Dahl family life, much as Roald would conclude that his own life had shrunk. Here was no space for a dark room, no studio for Louis, and Alfhild and Else's duets were consigned to memory. Only months before, driving from Alexandria to Haifa, Roald had exulted in the luxury of solitude. 'I had never before been totally without sight of another human being for a full day and a night,' he wrote, secure in his return to the unsettling but vivid routine of 'flying around [seeing] all sorts of horrible things happening', certain that busyness and purpose awaited him.[15] Now he lacked both. As much as when he lay unseeing in his hospital bed in Alexandria, his burned face bound in bandages, unable to move, Roald was in limbo. He turned his attention to his mother's garden, digging deep trenches for raspberry canes, preparing the ground thoroughly. 'Every year or two he would become immersed in a new hobby,' one of his daughters wrote later of a loosely fictionalized version of Roald.[16] In this instance, Roald needed more than a hobby. Soon gardening gave way to something entirely unexpected.

On 24 March 1942, Roald received a diplomatic identification card from the Foreign Office. Three days later, he set sail from Glasgow for Canada. His destination was the British Embassy in Washington. His appointment as assistant air attaché by Harold Balfour, Churchill's under-secretary of state for air, was one, he suggested, he had accepted reluctantly. In years to come, the minutiae of this twist of fortune did not concern Roald unduly – as he wrote in *The Minpins*, 'sometimes mysteries are more intriguing than explanations'.[17] Serendipity played its part: dinner at Pratt's, the gentlemen's club in London; at the single table in the club's basement dining room Balfour and Roald, who had not met before, seated next to one another.

The Washington that greeted Roald in the spring of 1942 was cheerful with cherry blossom. Shops, restaurants and taxis were all busy, wartime privations unthought of. In a country still volubly isolationist, opposed in many quarters to intervention in what was widely regarded as an overseas conflict, Roald's appointment was concerned with public relations. Tall, handsome, a uniformed RAF mannequin, his remit was to play his part in embassy efforts to promote US support for Britain's war effort. Beyond his good looks and attachment to the RAF it was an ill-fitting appointment for Roald, with his poor track record of esprit de corps, his casual brusquerie and strong sense of himself. A fighter pilot in North Africa and Greece, he had delighted in belonging to a fraternity bonded by purpose and shared risks, and his airborne autonomy. Like the empty chatter of the Dar es Salaam Club, the frigid hierarchies and stilted protocols of the British Embassy provoked Roald to speedy disgruntlement. He disliked the ambassador, Lord Halifax, a former viceroy of India, aloof and Edwardian, and he jibbed at expectations that he would fritter his evenings charming Washington's 'cocktail mob' or, like a latter-day bard, accepting 'boring invitations from social hostesses' in order to pass on anecdotes of pilots' derring-do.[18] Less than a year out of active service, he remained entrenched in a wartime mentality, cut off from embassy hands and 'po-faced, cod-eyed' party-going Americans by a gulf of harsh experience and stark reminders in the form of punishing headaches.[19] That he became as a result in his own words 'rather outspoken and brash' appears inevitable.[20] Here were grounds for the impatience with empty chatter that later led him to cut out of the *New York Times* a quotation from Jonathan Swift's 'Thoughts on Various Subjects' of 1706: 'The common fluency of speech in many men, and most women, is owing to a scarcity of matter'.[21] Small recompense were the duty-free whisky and diplomatic immunity from motoring fines of which he boasted to Sofie Magdalene, the ready availability of pre-war luxuries, like the boxes of chocolate he arranged to be sent at intervals to his mother and sisters, evenings of poker at the University Club or a routine that began at ten o'clock each morning, assisted by a Canadian secretary, and whenever possible, ended like his days in Tanganyika, with whisky and gramophone records and the consolation of his own company.

It was in Washington, however, that Roald discovered at first hand the power of his own storytelling. In a school essay about nursery rhymes he had commended the impact of bold narratives like those that had enthralled him at Sofie Magdalene's knee. In Washington, he himself became the storyteller, tasked with selling to hard-nosed isolationists a version of RAF bravery worth paying for. He undertook evening speaking engagements to politely detached audiences; and within days of his arrival, he met the first of the professional storytellers who, he claimed, changed his life.[22] Their encounter was unexpected and, initially, disappointing. The man himself was 'very small … with thick steel-rimmed spectacles', a hesitant shuffle and 'nothing in the least unusual about him'.[23] He appeared in Roald's office in the embassy annexe that housed the Air Mission, in pursuit of a flying story for the influential weekly magazine the *Saturday Evening Post*. He invited Roald to tell him his most exciting adventure over lunch; he revealed himself as the novelist C. S. Forester, then working in the

States for the British Ministry of Information. Suddenly Roald, who had read Forester since his schooldays, was 'churning with excitement'. As he recounted events thirty years later, excitement muddled him. He failed to give a good account of himself, distracted by smoked salmon and roast duck and partly, he explained, because 'I have never been much good at telling stories aloud'.[24] He offered to write down what had happened to him in the hours from his departure from Fouka and to send Forester his jottings for the novelist to rewrite, and the same evening he did just this in the comfort of his room in the Willard Hotel. He wrote quickly. At midnight, after five hours, the story was finished. Roald remembered its genesis as life-changing, akin to a mystical experience, a sensation like 'float[ing] back in time ... the hand that held the pencil mov[ing] back and forth across each page' as if invisibly propelled.[25] An astonished Forester did not consider rewriting it. Instead he passed it to his agent, Harold Matson, who sold it to the *Post* on Roald's behalf. It was published on 1 August over two pages, complete with colour illustration.

The *Saturday Evening Post* wanted propagandist reportage. While claiming it as 'a factual report on Libyan air fighting', it Americanized Roald's account to guarantee its readers' sympathies. Editors retitled the piece 'Shot Down Over Libya', a distortion and the only revision in which

Roald acquiesced. Perhaps its chipper film-voiceover style came to irritate him: 'It was getting hot in the cockpit. My shirt and pants were dark with sweat and I smelt like hell. You can't take a bath in four pints of water a day when you've got to use it for drinking as well, at least, I can't because I'm pretty big.'[26] For the most part Roald responded angrily to editorial interventions, undeterred by his own status as newcomer, uncowed by the *Post*'s Olympian clout. Later, still disgruntled, he rewrote the piece, restored its original title, 'A Piece of Cake', and included it in his collection of flying stories, *Over to You*. He told his mother that the magazine's editors had 'half ruined' his efforts.[27]

'All my adult life,' wrote Roald in 1988, 'I have worked alone in one small room ... I cannot suddenly adjust to ... listening to a dozen different people voicing their views.'[28] Metaphorically Roald shut himself into a room from which he excluded dissenting voices from the outset: his confidence in his work was immense and, as all his publishers would be forced to recognize, he never rated contradictory views as highly as his own. In this instance, he offered his mother a defensive-sounding apologia: the story was 'purely in my line of duty, because they say it does a lot of good with the American public'; with customary boastfulness, he added 'the *Saturday Evening Post* is the widest read magazine in America with a circulation of about 4 million. I am told that it's every author's ambition to get a story therein.'[29] Neither then, on the brink of his twenty-sixth birthday, nor at any point afterwards would publication alone satisfy Roald's vision of himself. He required his writing to be prominent, praised and, above all, profitable.

And he worked hard to these ends. He wrote carefully, for much of the time slowly; he researched thoroughly; and he set about his work with conviction. Published anonymously as an account by 'an RAF pilot at present in this country for medical reasons', 'Shot Down Over Libya' earned Roald $187.50, the commendations of Harold Matson and his mother's pride. Outwardly, Roald's life did not change. The change was within himself: a restored certainty that banished the shadow of his crash landing in the desert, and the troubling vision of ordinariness that had assailed him in Grendon Underwood, digging trenches for raspberry canes in his mother's garden while a distant war pursued its course without him.

In novel called *My Uncle Oswald*, published in 1979, Roald would suggest that at least one kind of success is acquired 'by chicanery, by talent, by inspired judgement or by luck'.[30] The vector for change in his own case was a forty-page manuscript inspired by RAF mythology that showcased his talent for vivid fantasy and tight plotting: what happened next was a combination of luck and, arguably, inspired judgement in accurately reading the zeitgeist. At the end of June, Roald told Sofie Magdalene that, in his lunch hour 'and in spare moments because I'm pretty busy', he had written 7,000 words about 'little types with horns and a long tail who walk about on the wings of your aircraft boring holes in the fuselage and urinating in your fuse-box'.[31] He described it as 'a sort of fairy tale'.[32] Its subjects were gremlins, characters '"well-known" by the entire RAF', in Roald's estimate 'a very real and considerable part of the conversation of every RAF pilot in the world'.[33] His decision to place them in a 'beautiful green wood far up in the North' points to his early steeping in Norse tales and his love of the country: his story begins 'in early autumn, when the chestnuts [are] ripening and the apples [are] beginning to drop off the trees' – September, his birthday month, which he called 'the Month of the Conker'.[34] Roald annotated inkblots on the same letter with the explanation 'a gremlin walked across the page after bathing in my ink bottle'; his gremlins wore suction boots and green bowler hats, like the Minpins in the last of his children's stories, who are 'curiously old-fashioned' in dress and '[walk] up and down almost vertical [tree] branches without the slightest trouble', wearing suction boots that resemble green wellingtons.[35] His absorption was whole-hearted, as his story of gremlin-like Minpins four decades later indicates; in his imagination, fact and fiction elided. In September, he claimed he 'really [did] know what [gremlins] look like, having seen a great number of them in my time'.[36] The recipients of such assurances were understandably wrongfooted.

With cheerful determination, Roald had set his sights on magazine publication. To Sofie Magdalene, he hazarded likely payment at $500, equivalent to around £125. Immersion in his fantasy of diminutive mischief-makers leavened June evenings in Roald's rented house in Georgetown, in north-west Washington. Writing was escapist, returning him to 80 Squadron: fleeting release from his headaches, which continued 'fairly active' throughout that summer, and the polished banalities of the embassy and his work for the Air Mission.[37] He wrote whenever he could, mostly in the evening.[38]

Without the intervention of a British businessman, founder of a cinema company in Dover, employed during the war at the New York-based British Information Services, 'Gremlin Lore' might have remained a whimsical wartime magazine piece. Sidney Bernstein read Roald's story and promptly dispatched it to Walt Disney. Bernstein had previously advised on the screenplay for MGM's blockbuster wartime romance *Mrs Miniver*, released to commercial and critical acclaim only weeks before Roald completed his typescript. Terms of Roald's employment required him to show material intended for publication to his superiors in both Washington and London. Several reacted to 'Gremlin Lore' with bafflement, but Bernstein identified in Roald's story propaganda as potent as *Mrs Miniver*. Walt Disney agreed. His interest in Roald's gremlins, described by Roald as a 'shock', was immediate. 'If he really means business,' Roald wrote to his mother, with a characteristic leap, 'it will become worth many thousands of dollars.'[39]

Recommending his collection of flying stories, *Over to You*, a reviewer in a provincial newspaper described Roald in 1946 as 'an onlooker who sees very colourful and rather unusual scenes', a verdict as accurate of Roald's gremlin story as his flying stories, and equally true of his accounts of his own life.[40] His first skirmish with Hollywood undoubtedly proved both colourful and unusual. At the outset the view of a Disney employee that Roald did 'not regard himself as a professional writer' was misleading in its suggestion of naivety.[41] As in his dealings with the *Saturday Evening Post*, Roald's response to Disney's overtures was assertive and unrelenting: he was still the very tall boy, arrogant, opinionated and stubborn, who had alienated masters at Repton. Disney himself responded positively to the young man's combination of brazen confidence and charm; unable to pronounce 'Roald', he called him 'Stalky'. Flattered, an excited Roald remained nevertheless determined to exercise tight control over any collaboration with the Hollywood giant. He had already decided to allocate profits to the RAF Benevolent Fund, beginning with wireless sets for squadrons in the Middle East.

The contract Roald eventually negotiated – helped by New York lawyer and general counsel to the Democratic National Committee Sol Rosenblatt – did indeed grant him high levels of control over any gremlins film made by Disney. In the meantime, Disney's practised publicity machine promoted its new project with gusto. Gremlin characters featured in advertisements, a comic strip appeared called 'The Three Little Gremlins', there were 'gremlin' hats and a big band tune by Buddy Tate, 'Dance of the Gremlins'; a version of Roald's story published in *Cosmopolitan* in December described its unnamed author as a 'noted gremlinologist'. The $50,000 spent by Disney over the next eighteen months included, in November 1942, a two-week visit by Roald, at Walt's invitation, to the company's Burbank studios and a second visit five months later. On both occasions Roald was put up in the Beverly Hills Hotel and provided with a car. He spent his days in meetings with Walt Disney or working alongside Disney artists to produce the illustrated storybook published in April 1943 as *The Gremlins*. In November, Walt threw a party for his newest protégé. Hollywood stars appeared as gremlins: Charlie Chaplin, Spencer Tracy, Dorothy Lamour and *Mrs Miniver* leading lady, Greer Garson. In contrast to his attitude to embassy-sponsored social life in Washington, Roald appeared determined to enjoy himself. 'All the girls went crazy for him,' one of Disney's illustrators remembered.[42] Roald's first fling was with an actress called Phyllis Brooks, shortly to retire from films at the age of thirty. His description for Sofie Magdalene of an evening spent with Ginger Rogers was coyly – or complacently – ambiguous. He flirted with Marlene Dietrich. As he had since school, he made sense of increasingly out-of-the-ordinary occurrences in the orderly narrative of his letters to his mother.

But in his relationship with his host, Roald apparently had no intention of acknowledging himself the junior partner. As in his dealings with the *Saturday Evening Post*, he dug in his heels in defence of what he had written. Disagreements focused on gremlins' appearances: the illustrations produced by Disney artists omitted both their tails and their green bowler hats. Roald resisted compromise; Disney himself set aside the younger man's objections. Not for the last time, Roald refused to concede defeat. His attitude was both proprietorial and protective, his story a hymn to his love of flying and his continuing loyalty to the RAF and his fellow pilots 'all born to fly, higher than the highest high'.[43] A copy of *The Gremlins* signed by Roald in June 1943 preserves his irritation and his intransigence. On the title page he altered the illustration for the book's recipient. 'There should be a bowler hat and a tail,' he wrote alongside it, and he added both with bold strokes of his pen. Yet fledgling author and Hollywood behemoth were unequal sparring partners: Roald was powerless to prevent Disney from abandoning the project. In December 1943, after protracted to-ing and fro-ing, Walt informed Roald there would be no film. American cinema-goers, polls suggested, had tired of war material.

Roald's brush with Hollywood transformed him into a published author and, in his agent's assessment, an 'almost instantaneous success'; it introduced him to a rarefied neverland of partying film stars; it convinced him of a role for himself in Anglo-American relations and the creative and commercial possibilities of his own imaginings.[44] For a young man inclined to self-importance, the chances of emerging unscathed were slight.

That Roald's behaviour fell foul of the embassy's code of polite restraint is no cause for surprise. He had only ever trimmed his behaviour in line with expectations within his own family or the RAF. Disappointed in his pilot's career, still troubled by his injuries, impatient of diplomatic niceties, convinced of his own special abilities and certain he deserved a level of recognition that embassy mandarins denied him, swaggering Roald ruffled feathers. To himself he explained his attitude to negotiations with Disney as motivated by a determination to obtain best possible terms for the RAF Benevolent Fund; Roald gave away the fees he received for short stories, including $1,000 received from the *Ladies' Home Journal* in November, which he gave to an RAF widow in Washington whose husband had been killed in a car crash. Yet among his colleagues in the Air Mission and beyond were those unaware of his habitual generosity, who preferred to castigate him as conceited and self-seeking.

Roald's Achilles heel, however, was to prove his trump card. His gremlins won him influential admirers. Among them were the president's wife, Eleanor Roosevelt, from whom Roald's present of a signed copy of his book for her grandchildren elicited an invitation to visit, and a maverick Hungarian film producer, Gabriel Pascal. Pascal had recently directed a successful film adaptation of Bernard Shaw's *Major Barbara*. In a reprise of Roald's first meeting with C. S. Forester, he unveiled his latest plan to Roald over lunch, having presented himself, uninvited and unknown, at his office. In Roald the gremlinologist Pascal decided he had discerned a kindred spirit: he asked him to write the screenplay for 'an enormous film about the world and good and evil'.[45] Pascal's own powerful supporters included the vice president, Henry Wallace. Lunch with Wallace followed the next day. Wallace reiterated Pascal's request that Roald write the film's script; politician and airman talked into the early evening. As Roald explained to his mother, so easily and unexpectedly did a twenty-six-year-old invalided flight lieutenant find himself 'in very high circles – so bloody high that sometimes it is difficult to see the ground'.[46]

In the event, following the death of its producer in a plane crash, Pascal's film came to nothing. By contrast, Roald's friendship with Wallace flourished. It brought him into contact with the man he would afterwards describe as his best friend in the world, a like-minded iconoclast, Charles Marsh. Thirty years Roald's senior, a self-made newspaper magnate turned philanthropist, Marsh was to become the father figure Roald had never had: brash, appealingly bombastic, self-important, public-spirited and, to Roald, witty, kind and extraordinarily generous.

V

THE PERFECT SPY?

1943–1950

'Trying to create amity.'

ROALD ONCE DESCRIBED 'spy' as 'an ugly word' and denied any connection with anti-American wartime surveillance in Washington. 'I was trying to create amity,' he explained. 'My job was to try to help Winston Churchill to get on with FDR [President Roosevelt], and tell Winston what was in the old boy's mind.'[1] In private, he was less inclined to equivocate; he was clear that his motives were patriotic. His second wife Liccy, privy to Roald's off-the-record recollections, has described him as 'definitely finding out information for the British government'. Given his eye and ear for detail, his sense of fair play, charm and loyalty, and an opportunistic streak in Roald, she labelled him 'the perfect spy'.[2]

On 17 June 1943, Roald sent Sofie Magdalene good news: he had been promoted to the rank of squadron leader.[3] A week later, his news was more startling: the president had invited him to spend the weekend at Hyde Park, Roosevelt's house in upstate New York; he regarded Roald, Roald suggested, as a friend of his wife's.[4] The 'very high circles' in which Roald found himself had reached an apogee: his fellow guests that weekend included Crown Princess Martha of Norway and her children Prince Harald and Princesses Astrid and Ragnhild. But this was to be more than a weekend of idle chatter or royal hobnobbing, with Roald, in his own words, playing the clown to disarm his wily host. In its aftermath he supplied British embassy officials with a ten-page report on his visit, as Roosevelt had surely known he would. At this stage Roald's links with Britain's intelligence community in the States were informal (and would remain so for another year): the closeness of Roald's friendship with Wallace, added to occasional access to the president, made him too useful a source of information to set aside lightly, even for those at the Air Mission least sympathetic to him, including his immediate boss, Air Commodore 'Bill' Thornton, and the new head of the RAF delegation, Air Marshal William Welsh, who nevertheless manoeuvred to bring about his dismissal within the year. A Russian speaker, conciliatory towards the Soviet Union and anti-British in his views, Henry Wallace was positioned as Roosevelt's successor. For Halifax and his staff, as for British politicians at home, this was a troubling prospect.

Despite their friendship, it was a prospect that troubled Roald, too. Roald also showed his report of his visit to Hyde Park to Charles Marsh, at whose house in Washington he most often encountered Wallace. Marsh was a committed Democrat; unsuccessfully he longed to be admitted to Roosevelt's inner circle; political gossip delighted him, and he admired Wallace. In sharing his report, Roald may have felt he was paying back a favour. Previously Marsh had shown Roald a draft copy of a discussion document by Wallace outlining post-war US foreign policy. At the heart of *Our Job in the Pacific* was American 'encouragement' of independence among Pacific region territories of the British Empire. On that occasion, Marsh appeared not to recognize the likely effect on Roald of the document he showed him: Roald regarded it as a cold-blooded body-blow aimed at Britain's overseas possessions, and traitorous on the part of an ally. In his own later account acting with both speed and stealth, he had arranged for the document to be secretly copied, while he explained its temporary absence, which lasted no more than fifteen minutes, by pretending he was trying to find somewhere quiet to read it. He told neither Marsh nor Wallace what he had done, but would claim subsequently that the copied document made its way to Churchill, whose response of 'cataclysms of wrath' was much the same as his own.[5] *Our Job in the Pacific* altered Roald's relationship with Wallace: although the men remained friends, Roald's subsequent vigilance was not a feature of conventional friendship. Roald's had become a double life. He was still the air attaché intent on promoting the RAF in Washington salons; at the same time he was a gatherer and conduit of information in Britain's best interests – as he explained his informal role, 'I'd slip [Halifax's senior adviser] a couple of bits of information which I thought might help the war effort', grounds for one intelligence chief's thanks, in a letter written in June 1945, for the 'many occasions [during the period of your attachment to the British embassy] when your cooperation – always unstintingly given – was of great use to us'.[6] Roald was excited by this careful balancing act and the adroitness with which, habitually indiscreet, he nevertheless maintained necessary secrecy, as well as by his commitment to what he regarded as a patriotic mission.[7] Excitement offered compensation of sorts for the loss of his pilot's career and served as a measure of the changes within him.[8] In a story called 'Someone Like You', written in 1944, he described a pilot who, like him, had been 'in the Western Desert ... in Greece ... at Habbaniya'.[9] In the pilot's attitude to his wartime career is no exulting or even relief at his own survival, only the disillusionment that follows his acknowledgement of his power to inflict death arbitrarily, a reflection of Roald's own retreat from more boisterous views on RAF heroism.

In truth, excitement was not in short supply for the handsome young airman whose direct manner, charm, brisk humour and growing literary reputation made him 'the most attractive man in Washington'.[10] Roald may have failed to make friends in the embassy staff: he amply compensated among the Americans he encountered – as well as Marsh and Wallace, a sequence of rich, well-connected, in some cases beautiful, older, invariably married women, including sexagenarian cosmetics entrepreneur Elizabeth Arden, congresswoman Clare Boothe Luce, whose husband owned *Time* and *Life* magazines, oil heiress Millicent Rogers and gold mine heiress Evalyn Walsh McLean, at whose dinner parties 'everything was gold. All the plates, all the knives, forks, spoons and salt cellars etc'.[11] Roald was fascinated by wealth: 'The rich are always interesting,' he stated baldly.[12] He was also candid about his enjoyment of sex, quoting George Bernard Shaw on 'the Pleasures of Man': 'eating, drinking, chatting, sexual intercourse'; sex, he suggested, far outweighed affection in a typical romantic relationship.[13] Repeatedly his social conquests became sexual conquests: 'I think he slept with everybody on the East and West Coasts that had more than fifty thousand dollars a year,' remembered Charles Marsh's daughter, Antoinette.[14] His letters to his mother detailed the vapidity of unvarying social encounters, trappings of his Washington acquaintances' riches, the efforts of ageing society women to cling to vestiges of youth. His response to his sexual conquests was complex: detachment from the women themselves, in some cases bordering on dislike, balanced by a connoisseur's relish for their sumptuous surroundings and deep pockets. He showed off gold trinkets given to him by Millicent Rogers; of Clare Boothe Luce, he told a friend, 'I am all fucked out. That goddamn woman has absolutely screwed me from one end of the room to the other for three goddam

ROALD DAHL

ROALD DAHL

congresswoman Clare Boothe Luce, whose husband owned *Time* and *Life* magazines, oil heiress Millicent Rogers and gold mine heiress Evalyn Walsh McLean, at whose dinner parties 'everything was gold. All the plates, all the knives, forks, spoons and salt cellars etc'.[11] Roald was fascinated by wealth: 'The rich are always interesting,' he stated baldly.[12] He was also candid about his enjoyment of sex, quoting George Bernard Shaw on 'the Pleasures of Man': 'eating, drinking, chatting, sexual intercourse'; sex, he suggested, far outweighed affection in a typical romantic relationship.[13] Repeatedly his social conquests became sexual conquests: 'I think he slept with everybody on the East and West Coasts that had more than fifty thousand dollars a year,' remembered Charles Marsh's daughter, Antoinette.[14] His letters to his mother detailed the vapidity of unvarying social encounters, trappings of his Washington acquaintances' riches, the efforts of ageing society women to cling to vestiges of youth. His response to his sexual conquests was complex: detachment from the women themselves, in some cases bordering on dislike, balanced by a connoisseur's relish for their sumptuous surroundings and deep pockets. He showed off gold trinkets given to him by Millicent Rogers; of Clare Boothe Luce, he told a friend, 'I am all fucked out. That goddamn woman has absolutely screwed me from one end of the room to the other for three goddam

109

nights.'[15] As a young man seduced by the forty-something wife of a family friend, one of Roald's fictional alter egos, Oswald Hendryks Cornelius, betrays a similar ambivalence. Oswald is torn between physical attraction that nevertheless reduces his partner to a collection of body parts – 'a torso that tapered to a waist I could have circled with my two hands', 'a jewelled hand', 'heaving' bosom – and, for the room in which he finds himself, a lingering appreciation that recalls Roald's own in similar circumstances. 'There was a Boucher pastel on one wall and a Fragonard watercolour on another,' notes the narrator of *My Uncle Oswald*, much as Roald had inventoried Millicent Rogers' collection of paintings in her house in South Virginia: 'In the next room there were twelve Boucher and some Fragonard. All very beautiful.'[16] Antoinette Marsh pinpointed arrogance as uppermost in Roald's treatment of the women she claimed 'just fell at his feet'; another friend observed his resistance to emotional entanglements.[17] His customary aloofness played its part. So, too, a certain tough cynicism about his presence in Washington mansions. Stronger than his personal response to Evalyn Walsh McLean, whom he dismissed as 'very peculiar', was his awareness of her usefulness socially: 'she runs a good [salon] ... and there are a lot of folks to see and that's my business'; some of these 'folk' included Washington power brokers with little attachment to their

British allies.[18] Roald did not, for example, lose sight of the importance of bolstering Clare Boothe Luce's late conversion to Anglophilia, given her influence as politician and publisher's wife and both husband and wife's track record of anti-imperialism and hostility to Churchill. As throughout his time in Washington, his private and working lives merged.

In October 1943, Roald wrote cryptically to Sofie Magdalene of a new job 'about which I'm afraid I can tell you nothing'.[19] This was formalized the following spring and began in June 1944. Before that, Roald returned briefly to London. He sat for his portrait by Matthew Smith, whom he had met in 1941 – displayed in a gallery in Haymarket, Smith's paintings, with their bold, Fauvist colours, had enthralled injured, footloose Roald, who traced the artist to a rundown London hotel to tell him so; Roald also acted as a chaperone of sorts to his literary hero, Ernest Hemingway. Roald and Hemingway had crossed paths in Washington: from the Air Mission, Roald had arranged a commission for Hemingway as an RAF correspondent, which secured the author a seat on a seaplane to Britain. In a letter to Eleanor Roosevelt, Hemingway's wife Martha Gellhorn described Roald's intervention as 'angelically helpful', a view she may have revised after Roald failed to secure a second seat for her.[20] In London, Roald's attitude to Hemingway fluctuated

– he was irritated, for example, at being kept waiting while the writer applied hair tonic for incipient baldness – but his respect for his writing remained 'overwhelming', and Hemingway's style, with its much-copied sparseness, was an important influence on Roald's early stories like 'Katina'.

Roald's employment by the New York-based British Security Coordination (BSC), a wartime secret service network, formalized his sideways step into intelligence. His involvement was not with covert, Bond-style espionage. Instead, he was deployed by BSC's director William Stephenson for purposes Roald described as 'oil[ing] the wheels'. Since 'theoretically I was a nobody', he explained, 'I could ask FDR over lunch what he thought, and he could tell me, quite openly, far more than he could say in a formal way.' In this way, Roald's work scarcely differed from aspects of his pre-BSC Washington life: his report on his weekend with the Roosevelts; his quick-fire decision to copy Wallace's foreign policy documents. What changed, however, was Roald's perception of the likely impact of his actions. 'Bleeding this information on the highest level from the Americans was not for nefarious purposes, but for the war effort,' he stated later.[21] Until his death, he resisted further explanation.

Yet despite his pleasure in his departure from the embassy, in the eighteen months until his return to Buckinghamshire

Roald's happiness was mixed. After-effects of his flying accident lingered: years later he was still conscious of 'an ache, or a pain, or a slight disability' that never receded fully.[22] In this instance, agonizing back pains first forced him to heavy doses of alcohol, then two operations, including removal of a disc. Charles Marsh paid for both and facilitated luxurious convalescence of the sort to which Roald had become accustomed in Alexandria: in Marsh's house in Virginia, paintings by Monet and Renoir vied for Roald's attention with an indoor staff of eighteen. Confined to bed for much of the time, Roald read 'a lot of that old stuff which I'd never read before': novels by the Brontës and Dickens – his absorption of Dickens's merging of fantasy and elaborate grotesquerie is evident in his own writing.[23] Happier was an intense, passionate, sexually adventurous affair with a French actress called Annabella, again Roald's senior, married to the film star Tyrone Power. Unusually for Roald's romantic life to date, the two recognized in one another a similarity of outlook that, more than sexual chemistry, underpinned their relationship. Annabella likened them to siblings in their attitudes: for all his sexual charisma, Roald was more practised in the role of brother than lover. Their affair ended with Power's return from the US air force. Annabella's later description of Roald as 'kind of impossible' was admiring and affectionate and the two remained close following Annabella's return to France and Roald's return to England: Roald would write to her candidly about his marriage difficulties.[24]

On a deeper imaginative and emotional level, Roald was sustained by his writing. In his letters to Sofie Magdalene, this had always been the case: consistently a lifeline, a plea for endorsement, applause, affection, and a private communing and ordering of his world. Wartime Washington convinced Roald that his writing *mattered*. His stories – 'Shot Down Over Libya', 'The Sword', 'Only This', 'Beware of the Dog', 'Someone Like You' or the Hemingway-esque 'Katina' – found markets and readers and earned Roald not only the fees that he passed on to RAF charities but a degree of public renown: Walt Disney's interest; a distinguished literary agent, Ann Watkins, whose clients included Hemingway and Dylan Thomas; Eleanor Roosevelt's admiration. In Washington, Roald's writing, like Roald, was in demand.

His homecoming in February 1946 turned back the clock. In one of Roald's stories of unhappy marriages, 'Neck', Sir Basil Turton is forced out of comfortable country bachelorhood into the hurly burly of a London characterized by Roald as sexually predatory. There, an aggressive, rapacious, calculating young woman speedily entraps him in an unsuitable marriage; she compels him to live his life on the public stage he has happily shunned. After years in the American capital – lionized, fêted and pursued – Roald's return to Buckinghamshire and the house he shared with his mother and sisters threatened to reverse the story of Sir Basil's emergence from rural obscurity; after visiting him there, Martha Gellhorn described the atmosphere as 'very boring and very heavy'.[25] Roald approached his thirtieth birthday unmarried and uncertain in his prospects. Supported by a middling sum from Harald's trust and an RAF pension, he determined to embrace Sofie Magdalene's ramshackle peacetime bucolia; he bought a greyhound for racing, acquired a pet magpie and once again set about growing fruit and vegetables. His daughter Tessa would reflect that Roald's head had been turned by rarefied social encounters in the States, his four years' steeping in millionaires' lives of ease and plenty; in suffering post-war Britain, despite parcels of food, kitchen gadgets and clothing sent to the Dahls by Charles Marsh's secretary, Claudia Haines, the contrast made him listless, then downcast. Uppermost in his thoughts was his writing. 'I have become quite excited about [writing] and writing stories is the only … thing that I want to do,' Roald had stated ahead of publication at the beginning of the year of *Over to You*.[26] Yet his whole literary success, including his signing by Ann Watkins, was rooted in America. Awareness of his lack of literary standing at home increased his sense of post-war bleakness. He had left Washington intent on writing an admonitory novel based on his fears of nuclear war. On completion in June 1947, *Some Time Never* was a disillusioned, sad, astringent book, full of Roald's unhappiness and pulled, like him, in different directions, part despondent, part uncomfortably frivolous. Its cast again included gremlins, in this instance shorn of any power to beguile and lacking benignity. Ann Watkins sold the novel in the States; at home, to Roald's fury, his new British agent, Peter Watt, acting on a reader's report, declined to read it. Although the novel *was* published on both sides of the Atlantic, its reception was at best lukewarm. Roald came to share this view, albeit his own verdict was coloured by his disillusionment at responses to the novel on the part of those who encountered it pre-publication, including Watt and publishers Hamish Hamilton. Later Roald referred to it as 'that ghastly book'.[27]

In its aftermath, Ann Watkins declined to humour Roald's requests that she find him journalistic work, including as a foreign correspondent. Roald was rudderless, denied the splash his stories' reception had appeared to guarantee any novel he might write, still struggling to adapt to peacetime.

War and the feelings it provokes, he would write, demand 'our whole attention'; by contrast, 'after it is over it is only a memory'.[28] In the meantime nothing eclipsed these memories' vividness or filled the void convincingly. 'Let's have some memories of sweet days,' implores the narrator of one of Roald's stories written then.[29] The memories the narrator summons are as distant as he can manage, of 'seaside holidays in the summer', a retreat into early childhood; he invites his mother to share in the act of remembering. In reality this, too, was not the comfort it might have been for Roald. Sofie Magdalene appeared as melancholy and morose as her son; she described Roald as 'not easy to live with'.[30] Seemingly without its customary loving ease, their reunion caused both to withdraw within themselves. As he had in the winter of 1944, awaiting an operation on his back, Roald again began drinking heavily. Sofie Magdalene too. Shortly after Roald's return, she had moved to a house outside Great Missenden called Grange Farm, where Roald turned a cottage into a writing room, complete with blinds at the windows, which he drew even in daylight to minimize distractions, as he would in his writing hut at Gipsy House. Together but apart, this arrangement rooted in practicalities served as a metaphor for mother and son's separation. From afar – and unsuccessfully – Ann Watkins encouraged Roald to cheerfulness.

It did not help that a clutch of new stories failed to attract any interest, turned down even by the American magazines Roald regarded as his champions. Not for the last time, he was seriously worried about money. For Roald this was doubly troubling. It had never been enough simply to write. Competitive, including with himself, he needed his writing to be successful, and calibrated his success in dollars. He suggested as much to Charles Marsh, to whom he wrote at least once a week; in the circumstances his statement to his wealthy benefactor that he preferred to pay his own way in life was a plaintive one, pointing to potential grounds for wounded pride as long as he remained dependent on his mother or Charles's kindness. Roald was less open in letters to Ann Watkins. Characteristically, he denied any faltering of confidence in the face of repeated rejections. Whatever the fate of *Some Time Never*, he told her, the act of writing was itself useful practice; in January 1948, he insisted, 'I shall continue to write and I truly believe that one day I shall produce a really first-class novel.'[31]

He was mistaken in the short term. Roald worked slowly on *Fifty Thousand Frogskins*. The novel took him two years, dilatoriness the result of oscillating conviction and lassitude, in turn a reflection of his low mental state: greyhound racing, which drained his finite resources, engaged him more consistently. The result was a discursive, murkily humorous account of rural chicanery heavily based on his own experiences, in particular his friendship with his mother's odd job man, Claud Taylor, greyhound fancier, poacher, trout tickler and rogue; it contained warning signs of the anti-Semitism of which he would be accused later and, like early drafts of several of his children's novels, flaws in its construction. Roald argued that 'if you live in the country, your work is bound to be influenced by it', and the earthy realism of much of his second novel represented a deliberate rejection of fantastical elements in *Some Time Never*.[32] Three years after completing it, Roald successfully extracted four episodes for inclusion in his second collection of short stories, *Someone Like You*. They demonstrate the calibre of writing of which he was capable. Pungent imagery foreshadows his later style, like his description in 'Mr Feasey' of the greyhound racing crowd: 'Sharp-nosed men and women with dirty faces and bad teeth and quick shifty eyes. The dregs of the big town. Oozing out like sewage from a cracked pipe and trickling along the road through the gate and making a smelly little pond of sewage at the top end of the field.'[33] But the novel as a whole was unpublishable. Ann Watkins dismissed it as dull.

Roald had posed for publicity photographs with Walt Disney, the two men holding gremlin-inspired cuddly toys; he had lunched, dined, weekended with the president and first lady and, at the Norwegian Embassy in Washington, found himself a guest of the crown prince and princess; three of his stories had been broadcast on the BBC, another published in the *New Yorker*. But his first novel came close to failure and his second failed spectacularly. For Roald, it was a watershed moment, from which he was powerless to extricate himself. Later, in a version of the story that became *Matilda*, he would claim that 'most of the things we are frightened of are not really there at all. We just imagine they are'; he identified learning this lesson as 'one of the most important truths anyone can ever learn about life'.[34] Early in 1951, failure for Roald was more than an imaginative figment. In his own words to Ann Watkins, he fled. He fled from failure, fled from Britain, fled from his mother's house. He flew to Beirut to meet Charles Marsh. Marsh came to Roald's rescue with an offer of a job at his charity, the Public Welfare Foundation, an invitation to treat as his own Marsh's house in New York and, during a stopover in Cairo, a rich man's present of 'a beautiful alabaster [statue] made in at least 6000 BC and very valuable'.[35] 'Your spirit is with me now and tomorrow and yesterday,' Marsh had told Roald in the summer of 1945, assuring him of the strength of their friendship.[36] Five years after Roald's departure, the older man – Svengali turned fairy godmother – made good his promise, and Roald returned to the United States.

Left Roald – aged three and already tall for his age – with his mother, Sofie Magdalene, the towering figure of his childhood, in the gardens of Ty Mynedd, *c*.1919.

Above Dressed for the holidays, Roald with his sisters (from left: Asta, Else and Alfhild), *c*.1924.

Left 'Our life together was the stuff of which movies are made,' filmstar Patricia Neal would claim of her marriage to Roald. In 1953, their honeymoon destinations included Rome.

Above At home in Great Missenden in 1962, Pat and Roald and their three eldest children: from left, Theo, Tessa and Olivia.

Below All smiles in 1964, a year before Pat's strokes irreversibly altered the pattern of Roald's family life.

Dolphins and a Bacchic herm ornament this elaborate eighteenth-century
mirror, one of several Roald restored after learning how to water gild.

Roald at sixty, physically a little dented,
his imagination still vibrant.

Right In this uncertain image from 1960 of Roald with Tessa and Olivia are few signs of the vigour of Roald's doting parenting.

Below More than twenty years his junior, Felicity ('Liccy') Crosland would become the second Mrs Roald Dahl in 1983.

Below 'I long to sit quietly in Gipsy House, which I adore,' wrote Roald, of the house he and Pat bought in 1954, which remained his home until his death.

Above Roald, his grandson Luke and a gipsy caravan-shaped birthday cake, in the shadow of Roald's writing hut at Gipsy House.

Above Worldwide fame took Roald across the world. In 1988, he signed books at a children's bookshop in Amsterdam. *Below* Roald's partnership with Quentin Blake began in 1976 and lasted beyond Roald's death.

Above 'So Matilda's strong young mind continued to grow, nurtured by the voices of all those authors who had sent their books out into the world like ships on the sea. These books gave Matilda a hopeful and comforting message: You are not alone.' Illustration by Quentin Blake. *Below* 'The only nice and jumbly Giant in Giant Country': the BFG as pictured by Quentin Blake.

VI

MY LADY LOVE,
MY DOVE
1951–1957

'Almost enveloped by her ...'

FLASHES OF LIGHTNESS leaven the grim humour of a story about a husband and wife who decide to become card sharps that Roald wrote in New York in 1951. In 'My Lady Love, My Dove', the marriage of Arthur and Pamela is typically lopsided, the wife domineering, the husband deeply in thrall to her, but their relationship lacks menace, and even the prospect of being 'almost enveloped by her' does not unnerve Arthur unduly: he imagines it 'as though she were a great tub of cream and I had fallen in'. Playfully Roald even toyed with satire at his own expense. 'I myself do not like tall men,' diminutive Arthur tells the reader: 'they are apt to be supercilious and omniscient.'[1] Distant from the scene of his failure, temporarily disabused of claims to omniscience, Roald set his story in a comforting world of inherited wealth, a house with servants and gardeners, titled relations, no pressure of paid employment.

The *New Yorker* bought 'My Lady Love, My Dove' late that spring. Shortly before, the magazine had bought a story by Roald called 'Taste' about an impossible bet among wine buffs. Within a year, it would initiate an arrangement that secured it first refusal of Roald's subsequent short stories, paying Roald an honorarium of $100 for the privilege. If Roald was unhappy in his dependence on Charles Marsh, he could not help but be encouraged by this revival in his writing. To his mother, who, despite recent fractiousness, was missing him, Roald explained that pressure of work prevented him from leaving New York: 'I've got to stay on for a bit because there is a prospect of a fairly large contract for all my stories on radio and television.'[2] He had also received new scriptwriting offers and was working on radio adaptations of short stories by Somerset Maugham. His letters to Sofie Magdalene balanced customary boastfulness with concern for her wellbeing. In his self-appointed role of paterfamilias, he did his best to allay her concerns, solicitous about her ongoing dealings with Harald's trustees, a proposed move to an annexe of Else's house in Great Missenden, even her telephone bill. He forwarded advice from Charles about Sofie Magdalene's investments – 'If you will only do a little of what he suggests, your income should be increased a good bit' – and he reassured her about his own finances, stating that, though 'living in New York is terrifically expensive', he had saved £2,000 in less than a year since his return; he assured her that only a need to make money kept him there.[3] Once her house move was imminent, Roald instructed his mother which of his possessions to sell, requesting 'my desk I would like to keep, also the books', a clear statement of his priorities.[4] He sent her a present of Roman glass, which he was confident could be sold successfully, and he updated her on the progress of his own occasional art dealing, writing in May, 'It looks as though that Madonna picture

I cleaned up and repainted so much may fetch quite a bit over here, maybe even about $2,000.'[5] Roald had bought and sold paintings since the war, beginning with Epstein watercolours. Like greyhound racing and gambling, the art market's cunning and legerdemain appealed to him; he had also inherited his father's passion for art. In the 1940s, paintings by well-known artists were more affordable than they would become, and many of the first pictures Roald sold, including a Renoir, a Degas and a Sisley, paintings by Matisse, Cézanne, Bonnard and Soutine, were bought for his own pleasure with the proceeds of a short story, 'then because it took me so long to write another story, I would invariably have to sell the picture I had bought six months before'.[6] Of the artists in the collection of connoisseur Lionel Lampson in Roald's story 'Nunc Dimittis', written in 1953, he himself had owned paintings by several, among them Redon, Vuillard and his friend Matthew Smith.[7]

Roald was less forthcoming about his personal life. In the second half of 1951 he offered his mother so few details about a relationship with a Hungarian divorcée called Suzanne Horvath – despite apparently anticipating marrying Suzanne – that Sofie Magdalene, who 'never criticised her grown-up children, however much they deserved it', resorted to writing to Claudia Haines for information, rather than upbraiding Roald for his silence.[8] Roald prevaricated. He told his mother that he and Suzanne were 'not hurrying over getting married'; then he suggested their marriage would not be for a considerable time; then he reported that Suzanne had ended their relationship.[9] He offered neither explanation nor any indication of his feelings. He ought to have known – indeed, must have known – that this attitude would hurt Sofie Magdalene. At the end of the year, he embarked on a new relationship, but continued to drip-feed his mother only chicken fodder details.

Throughout Roald's fiction, marriage is flawed, unequal, even hazardous. In a story called 'Mrs Bixby and the Colonel's Coat', he referred to 'this terrifying pattern of divorce and death' that is a husband's lot; other stories crackle with husbands' cruelty to their wives and wives' resentment.[10] Successful marriages, like that of Anna Greenwood and Ed Cooper in 'The Last Act' or the boy-narrator's parents in *The Witches*, are cut short by road accidents, as his own parents' marriage had ended in Harald's early death; the cast-iron union of Mr and Mrs Fox is consistently threatened by Boggis, Bunce and Bean's machinations; in *George's Marvellous Medicine* and *The Magic Finger*, the amiable partnerships of George's parents and Mr and Mrs Gregg are of no interest to narrator or reader. Although Roald had been brought up with a strong sense of family, his exposure to successful marriage was negligible. Sofie Magdalene's protracted widowhood, Charles Marsh's serial marriages and Roald's own freewheeling sexual conquests – his power over women, 'ridiculously easy, like manipulating puppets', as he described sexual charisma in a late story for adults – appeared to deny him convincing evidence of marriage as either happy or supportive.[11] By the time the relationship on which he embarked late in 1952 moved towards marriage, Roald's expectations were as blunted as those of the weary spouses of his fiction.

Doubts linked Roald Dahl and film star Patricia Neal – the doubt each felt about their compatibility, their unspoken doubts about the trajectory of their shared future. Roald was thirty-six when they met in September at a dinner party organized by playwright Lillian Hellman, in whose play, *The Children's Hour*, Pat had recently been cast; on and off he had lived alone for twenty years. Ten years his junior, Pat was in love with fellow actor Gary Cooper. 'I'd have married him if he'd let me but he didn't want tying down and it was he who called it quits,' she admitted; their affair, which began in 1949, had lasted three years.[12] Neither Roald nor Pat was looking for the other; both, Roald suggested, were 'eager to get married'.[13] Pat's eagerness to have children was quickened by an abortion forced on her by Cooper; the photographs of Else's children Roald showed her convinced her of their likelihood of beautiful offspring. In her own words Pat was 'a spoiled Hollywood actress'.[14] Roald was sophisticated, generous, vigorously certain in his opinions, in Pat's assessment lean and handsome and 'interested in everything', in his own, unsentimental way[15]; he knew, too, that Charles Marsh enthusiastically seconded his mother's hopes for his marriage. When they met, Roald had ignored Pat. She was predictably irritated: when he telephoned the following morning, she turned down his invitation to dinner. Two days later he called again. That she acquiesced was almost certainly against her better judgement. To his mother, Roald would describe them both as cautious. Pat admired Roald, and Roald was attracted to Pat; he was not in love with her. Both apparently recognized the pragmatism that neither voiced. To his surprise Pat turned down Roald's first proposal, then changed her mind. Charles Marsh provided an engagement ring, in Roald's account a yellow sapphire of twenty carats, in Pat's a coloured diamond. Friends cautioned Pat against what they were convinced was a mistake; one wrote that her engagement ring was all that she would gain from the relationship. In her autobiography, Pat described an argument before their wedding: she accused Roald of arrogance, rudeness, nastiness.[16] It would not be the last time.

Neither of their families was present at their marriage ceremony in New York on a blistering July day in 1953: 'The furthest anyone came was from Brooklyn,' Roald remembered.[17] That night Roald told Pat he loved her. Pat responded with unhappy tears. They spent their honeymoon driving through Italy and France in an open-top Jaguar that repeatedly broke down. Their responses to what they saw spelled out their differences. Roald dissembled the extent of first disillusionment – he would tell a friend later that he did not display emotions: 'They may churn madly inside, but I always keep them there'[18] – yet disillusioned he undoubtedly was. Pat's claim that he was 'all set to leave [her]' after six months is supported by the letter Roald wrote to Charles Marsh in January 1954, in which he outlined at length the marriage's inherent weaknesses.[19] These included their fondness for 'different people, and also different things' and, more critically, Roald's belief that Pat was failing in her duties towards him as a wife: 'I make the coffee in the morning. She stays in bed. I work till lunchtime. Then I get my own lunch out of a can of soup.'[20] It was more than a response of its time. Roald both revelled in and struggled with Pat's fame. Previously, older women – rich, successful and prominent, like Clare Boothe Luce and Millicent Rogers – had spoiled their handsome trophy airman, their wealth a prop to his own conviction of his success. To Sofie Magdalene, Pat described her efforts to give Roald space for his writing in their New York apartment. Beyond this, as she admitted later, she 'never got him breakfast, never did any of the things that a European wife does to keep her man'.[21] She spent her mornings in bed on the telephone; her cooking skills were non-existent. A disaffected Roald set about an attempted seduction of Gloria Vanderbilt, which he shortly abandoned.

More straightforwardly successful was the book Roald published that autumn, his first for five years. A second collection of his short stories, including the quartet of stories salvaged from *Fifty Thousand Frogskins*, *Someone Like You* dazzled its veteran publisher, Alfred Knopf, impressed reviewers and quickly achieved sales of the sort Roald had dreamed of. Gratifyingly in the face of recent rejections, the book had been instigated by Knopf himself, who approached Ann Watkins after reading the opening story, 'Taste', in the *New Yorker*. Author and publisher were delighted with one another. A gourmet and wine collector, egotistical, swaggering, enthusiastic and larger than life, Knopf fitted the template of American success that had become Roald's lodestar. 'Americans are not impressed by understatement. It is not in their character,' he asserted later.[22] Nor, he might have added, was it in his own in matters concerning his writing.

It was not the mollifying effect of success that persuaded Roald to give his brief marriage a second chance. This was Charles Marsh's doing, in one of his last acts of friendship for Roald. In January 1954, Roald and Pat joined Charles and his former secretary, now his third wife, Claudia, in Jamaica. The Dahls had travelled separately, Pat first, Roald days later, initially unsure whether to follow the wife from whom he felt such distance. To each separately Charles gave loving, no-nonsense advice; to Roald, as so often before, he offered reassurance and invigoration – like Willy Wonka demolishing the Buckets' fears in *Charlie and the Great Glass Elevator*: 'You'll never get anywhere if you go about what-iffing.'[23] Pat agreed to defer to Roald; Roald lessened his expectations of Pat's domestic role. To Roald, although her own earnings greatly exceeded his, Pat handed control of the couple's finances, which she claimed achieved an instantaneous lessening of tension. Pat's subsequent description of her marriage as 'the first American house … where the woman didn't dominate' indicates that she kept her resolution; 'dominance' would be a criticism repeatedly levelled at Roald by his detractors.[24] The holiday ended in disarray nevertheless: Charles was bitten by a mosquito and contracted cerebral malaria, which set in train a succession of minor strokes. Although none of them suspected it at the time, it hastened a slow decline in his health from which he never recovered. While Claudia supervised Charles's nursing, Roald and Pat returned to New York. There, they visited a gynaecologist, who treated the blocked fallopian tubes that he identified as responsible for Pat's failure to conceive.

In old age, Roald would claim that he had 'never lived in a town or city in my life and I would hate to do so'.[25] Although inaccurate, the statement was an honest reflection of his attachment to the country: he regarded himself, like Danny's father in *Danny the Champion of the World*, as 'a true countryman': 'the fields, the streams, the woods and all the creatures who lived in these places were a part of his life'.[26] He had told Sofie Magdalene that his return to the States was financially motivated; his quest for success played its part. He had run away from *Fifty Thousand Frogskins* and the shattering of his vision of himself as a successful writer; he remained in thrall to the thrifty, crafty, beautiful rural world from which the novel emerged. Now he wanted to return. His marriage's near failure contributed to his disaffection with New York; Charles Marsh's illness, which left him unable to speak, lessened Roald's ties to the States. Although it would take several years and a near fatal accident for Roald to persuade Pat to move to Britain full time, she accepted his suggestion that they begin by spending part of every year in the same corner of Buckinghamshire as Sofie Magdalene and his sisters. Later, his daughter Tessa traced other motives on her father's part. In a loosely autobiographical novel, she claimed he 'thought he could prise [his wife] away from America, teach her about antiques, art and wine and then perhaps he could overlook the actressy part of her'.[27] Pat may have come to share this view. The memory of her preserved by a neighbour's child – 'Patricia Neal was so glamorous, she wore high heels and a fur coat … she smelt wonderful' – does not suggest overwhelmingly rural instincts.[28]

Roald described the acquisition of Gipsy House, his home for the rest of his life, with straightforward matter-of-factness that suggests the inevitability of a fairytale. 'My family wrote and told me that a small Georgian house with five acres was coming up for auction in Great Missenden. I wrote back asking them to try to get it for us. They bought it at auction in the village pub for £4,250. We paid half ourselves and borrowed the rest from my mother.'[29] The house chosen for Roald by Sofie Magdalene and Else was a small, white-painted square building, with four rooms downstairs, three bedrooms and a bathroom under its dark slate roof, tall white chimneystacks and outbuildings of brick and dun-coloured rubble. Long years of renting to tenant farmers accounted for its neglect: in the kitchen a flagged floor was laid unevenly on to earth, fireplaces offered the only heating, and the abandoned garden, Roald wrote, resembled 'a shambles'. But its orchard was full of apple and pear trees, a boon for Roald, for whom it was 'a most marvellous thing to be able to go out and help yourself to your own apples whenever you feel like it', and the house stood within walking distance of Great Missenden's narrow high street, close to his married sister Else, with whom Sofie Magdalene now lived.[30] Its large garden and position on the village perimeter, on a gentle incline that traced the path of an ancient drove road, appeared to safeguard its privacy. Roald and Pat arrived in the middle of May 1954, when 'the hawthorn was exploding white and pink and red along the hedges and the primroses were growing underneath in little clumps, and it was beautiful'; they supervised building work that included raising doorways for Roald's comfort and removing internal walls downstairs.[31] They moved in at the end of July. They renamed the house Little Whitefields. Rustic home-making made them both happy: at some point during their stay, Pat fell pregnant. Although Roald was disappointed during his visit by the lack of personal attention he received from Secker & Warburg, the British publishers of *Someone Like You*, reviews of the book, which appeared in April, were as encouraging as those in America. Roald was hailed as 'a genuinely Anglo-American writer'. In a statement he read with ambivalence, a reviewer reminded readers that 'Mr Dahl is the husband of actress Patricia Neal.'[32]

And so he would remain for some years. Throughout the 1950s, Pat continued to win both critical acclaim and widespread popularity, while Roald's career lurched between triumph and disaster. Following *Someone Like*

You, in January 1954 the *New Yorker* published a new story by Roald, 'The Way Up to Heaven'; five years would pass before the magazine accepted another. Twice during this interval, it rejected a story that has since become one of his best known. Roald worked on 'William and Mary', originally called 'Abide with Me', for nine months, a macabre vignette about a pettifogging husband whose brain and a single eyeball are kept alive after his death in 'a biggish white enamel bowl about the size of a wash-basin' in order to spy on his widow.[33] The trouble Roald took over the story's construction, especially its medical minutiae, suggests his primary focus was not his narration of the revenge on her excessively controlling husband of a wife depleted by 'years and years of joyless married life'; the story is not a fictionalizing of tensions within his own marriage.[34]

'William and Mary's failure to find a market, within months of the success of *Someone Like You*, may have encouraged Roald to cling to the earlier book. In the summer of 1954, he began writing a play that incorporated vignettes from three of its short stories – in his notes, he described its plot as '"Lamb to the Slaughter" with small changes'.[35] Shaped by Roald's teasing conviction that 'many women in this world would gladly murder their husbands if they thought they could get away with it', the play, which he called *The Honeys*, traced the course of three marriages, all of which ended with the husband's murder by his wife ('rather a sweet little thing'). In Britain, *The Stage* announced the project on 7 October, mistakenly describing it as a collaboration between Roald and the playwright Frederick Knott, author of *Dial M for Murder*, which that year had been released as a film directed by Alfred Hitchcock; the paper's headline – 'New Knott Thriller' – points to Roald's standing in his home country.[36] Instead, working on his own at the unfamiliar task of playwriting, Roald devoted two years to *The Honeys*. It occupied him throughout Pat's pregnancy with their first child, Olivia; to Pat's chagrin he was absent from Olivia's birth in New York on 20 April 1955, on tour with *The Honeys* in Boston. Both its Broadway run and a provincial tour flopped, but Roald agreed nevertheless to a British production the following year, which necessitated rewriting and a new title, *Your Loving Wife*, intended to pinpoint the piece's black humour. Despite this, and a cast headed by the popular Hermione Baddeley, the play garnered mixed reviews in Birmingham, Oxford and Bournemouth, and its London run was cancelled. A chastened Roald returned to New York. In October 1956, for the second time, Roald abandoned the scene of failure.

Absent parents fill Roald's fiction: a mother or father dead, or, like the Wormwoods in *Matilda* and Billy's mother in *The Minpins*, uninterested in their children, or otherwise preoccupied, like the Krankys in *George's Marvellous Medicine* and Charlie Bucket's overworked mother and father, or simply distant, like the mother in a story called 'The Wish', 'far away ... looking for her son', unaware of his fears and torments.[37] Overwhelmingly his heroes and heroines are parentless. 'No one is going to be worrying too much about me', the orphan Sophie tells the BFG: the statement applies in equal measure to any number of Roald's fictional offspring, beginning with Lexington, the 'beautiful baby boy' born 'once upon a time, in the City of New York' in a cautionary tale from 1960 called 'Pig'.[38] It would not be a criticism that, as children, Olivia, Tessa, Theo, Ophelia or Lucy Dahl could level against their father.

In October 1938, Sofie Magdalene had received a letter from a friend travelling, like Roald, on the SS *Mantola* to Africa. Describing Roald as 'very popular with everyone', she added, 'Luckily for him he is fond of children & is good with them, for they swarm all over him.'[39] Two decades later, Sofie Magdalene was able to judge for herself something of this observation's accuracy. Roald was thirty-eight when Pat conceived their first child and immediately excited by the prospect of fatherhood. By contrast, Pat would find she struggled as a mother, at one point handing over year-old Olivia to her sister-in-law Else for a period of several weeks. In her autobiography, she remembered Roald as 'a very maternal daddy'; her career offered lengthy periods of respite from Olivia, then Tessa, who was born two years later.[40] Despite a relish for the scatological that peppers his writing, Roald did not enjoy what he labelled newborns' 'whirling blur of wet nappies and vomit and milk and belching and farting'; he employed and oversaw a sequence of nurses.[41] But his letters written at this time reveal his familiarity with these aspects of childcare: more often than not, it was Roald, not Pat, who ministered to the family that, with Theo's birth in July 1960, had grown to three.

This succession of new babies interrupted Roald's writing. In New York, he rented a writing room in an apartment close to the Dahls' own; in the garden of Little Whitefields, as he had at Grange Farm, he converted an outbuilding to provide a quiet, cut-off place for working. There he could escape from being 'an ordinary fellow who walks around and looks after his children and eats meals and does silly things'; inspired by Dylan Thomas's converted wooden garage on a Carmarthenshire cliff, the white-painted, brick-built shed served as his writing hut until his death.[42] Working there in the summer of 1957, still smarting from *The Honeys*' baleful fate, Roald confronted a further, more challenging dilemma: in April, Alfred Knopf had expressed considerable disappointment in a new collection of short stories that included Roald's last two pieces published in the *New Yorker*, 'Edward the Conqueror' and 'The Way up to Heaven'. 'I couldn't possibly be less than frank with you,' Knopf had written. He made clear his grounds for reservation; he offered to publish the collection as it stood, but presented Roald with an alternative: 'I would like to see you hold it over a bit and strengthen it with at least two more stories right out of the top drawer.'[43] Accustomed to respond bullishly to criticism of his writing, Roald accepted this suggestion, a measure of his respect for Knopf. Progress, however, proved appallingly slow. 'The pencil doesn't very often touch the paper,' he commented once on his technique. 'It's looking and musing and correcting and then, then you do a little writing.'[44] That it would take him two more years to produce the required top-drawer stories dampened his appetite for short story writing for the next decade and beyond.

Published on both sides of the Atlantic in 1960, *Kiss Kiss*, as the collected stories were titled, replicated the pattern of Roald's previous collections: despite good reviews and positive publicity, American enthusiasm outstripped that of British readers. In June, *The Sunday Times* reprinted in full 'The Way up to Heaven': advertised in regional papers, the story was described as 'a minor masterpiece', 'in the tradition of O. Henry and Maupassant' and 'a contribution to holiday reading not to be missed'.[45] Among the eleven stories was evidence of the encroachment on Roald's imagination of children and parenthood: parental fears about babies' feeding in 'Royal Jelly', bigger fears about parental responsibility in the dark-hued 'Genesis and Catastrophe', which reimagined the birth of Hitler as a longed-for blessing for a sorrowing and downtrodden mother. Other stories point to ongoing preoccupations. 'The Champion of the World' is a pheasant-poaching tale that returns to the world of *Fifty Thousand Frogskins*; Roald would revisit it twenty years later in *Danny the Champion of the World*, but his first version was still an adults-only affair. A story called 'The Landlady' began as an attempt to write a ghost story of the sort Roald had loved since St Peter's, 'but when it was finished and I examined it carefully, I knew … I hadn't brought it off. I simply hadn't got the secret. So I … altered the ending and made it into a non-ghost story.'[46] Ghost stories were on his mind. Years before, Alfred Hitchcock had bought television rights to a handful of Roald's stories. In 1958, Roald embarked on a similar initiative with Alfred Knopf's film director half-brother, Edwin: 'a television series … of nothing but ghost stories.'[47] As with the writing of his own stories, he researched exhaustively. 'A tremendous amount of scuttling around' included visits to the British Library and to an elderly ghost story aficionado, the former royal biographer Lady Cynthia Asquith. Over a year Roald collected twenty-four and wrote a screenplay for the pilot episode: a story by E. F. Benson in which a Catholic priest's refusal to compromise the sanctity of the confessional shapes an unhappy outcome. Studio bosses were unanimous in their rejection of a piece almost certain to provoke America's powerful Catholic lobby; Roald described their 'apoplectic' response as a shock that stayed with him.[48]

How often, it seemed then, he had found himself at a crossroads: disappointed by the reception of *Some Time Never*; despondent following his failure with *Fifty Thousand Frogskins*; wrong-footed by repeated difficulties in finding a market for his stories; denied the screenwriting success he had anticipated from adapting ghost stories. In their wake, these setbacks brought other worries, too. On 27 June 1957, casting about to help him, Sheila St Lawrence, who had become Roald's point of contact at the Watkins Agency following Ann Watkins's retirement, suggested 'we could always ask for an advance from Knopf on the new collection'.[49] But in the summer of 1957, the new collection was still two years from completion to Alfred Knopf's satisfaction, and there would be no advance to help Roald's finances. Happily, Pat remained in demand in New York and Hollywood, but Roald struggled with the disparity in their professional fortunes. His instincts were exuberant, generous, acquisitive: at fortnightly auctions hosted by Restell's in the City of London, he filled the back of an old Morris station wagon with cases of 'good burgundy and claret ... for less than one pound a case';[50] he showered on his family what Else remembered as 'sacks full of presents'[51]; he delighted in 'haunt[ing] small auctions all over the country and com[ing] home with my old van loaded with canvases' and, as he had since the purchase of Little Whitefields, he hurried to 'exciting furniture auctions ... in vast decaying country houses all around'.[52] Like the 'houseproud wife' in his rewriting of 'Goldilocks and the Three Bears', he 'collected lovely things / Like gilded cherubs wearing wings, / And furniture by Chippendale / Bought at some ... auction sale'.[53] On its own, it was not enough. He had reached an impasse. He would provide the solution himself.

VII

MARVELLOUS MEDICINE

1957–1965

'And a crazy man running it?'

'D O YOU REMEMBER talking about a children's book you had in mind?' Sheila St Lawrence wrote to Roald on 5 June 1957.[1] Six weeks had passed since Alfred Knopf had informed Roald that the stories he had submitted for consideration as *Kiss Kiss* inspired 'a feeling of let-down'.[2] St Lawrence's motives were compassionate and canny. 'I know you are worried and deeply concerned at the Knopf and *New Yorker* reactions,' she continued; but she had read *The Gremlins* and discerned in what she called Roald's 'fantasy writing' a rewarding, almost certainly profitable way forward for an author whose career, despite successes, continued to falter. Emolliently she told Roald that *The Gremlins*' popularity 'would indicate that you have a bent in this direction and a ready audience to welcome such a book'. She suggested that the short story format that had served him well had become 'imprisoning'. Roald ignored her.

His change of heart was gradual. In one of his ideas books, on a page headed 'People', Roald experimented with imagery to describe faces, each simile a foreshadowing of the style of his later children's books: 'A pale grey face like a bowl of porridge', 'A face like an old sea boot', 'A nose like a bathroom tap/the tap in the bathroom', 'A small crooked mouth, shaped like a keyhole'.[3] Once ideas for short stories had dotted the books' lined pages: 'Do a murder with the leg of lamb from the deep freeze' ('Lamb to the Slaughter');

'The woman who stuck her head through a Henry Moore & couldn't get it out' ('Neck'); 'The pornographic bookseller who watches for the death of clergymen, then sends widow a bill and list of porno books' ('The Bookseller').[4] In their place appeared the kernels from which children's books would emerge, like the note on a 'boy who tips up glass', to which Roald added, 'Jimmy felt a little peculiar. Had he done it? Had he really?', a precursor to *Matilda*.[5] Once, as if ready now to cross this creative Rubicon, Roald wrote, 'It's time to do a children's book,' and the idea with which he toyed transported him back more than thirty years to 'The Kumbak II', in which Uncle Aristotle's listening machine enabled the solving of a murder: 'A murder handbook. A boy and a girl become murder detectives.'[6] In fact, the children's book on which Roald embarked, encouraged on and off by Sheila St Lawrence for the better part of a decade in what she called her 'letters in 1950–51–52 hounding you to do just such a book', came closest to a note for a story about an enormous cherry: 'Man who grew cherry the size of a grapefruit'.[7]

It was not an accident that much of Roald's preliminary thinking about the story that became *James and the Giant Peach* happened in Norway. In the summer of 1959, the Dahls, with their nanny Susan Denson, were on holiday. For Roald, magic swirled through the contours of the familiar landscape, shaped by his memories of childhood holidays and redolent of Sofie Magdalene's storytelling and the myths of the north, complete with giants and uncontrollable natural forces, shape-shifting, metamorphoses and the lurking menace of land, sea and sky. Once Norway had been a catalyst for Roald's childhood happiness; now, in the company of Pat and the two infant daughters to whom he would dedicate the story, it provided succour again. In the orchard at Little Whitefields, Roald had found himself looking at a cherry tree. What would happen, he wondered, if the cherries were to grow and grow and not stop growing? He asked the same question about apples and pears. And then he thought of a peach. He thought about animals, too. To his daughter Ophelia he would later explain his decision to write about 'little things like earthworms and centipedes and spiders' as shaped by a conviction that Beatrix Potter and A. A. Milne had already centred stories on other animals: 'I remember saying to myself, "I don't want creatures that have been used before in children's books. I don't want bunny rabbits or squirrels or Mr Toad or little mice. I want new creatures.'[8] Roald did not begin writing straightaway. This came afterwards, following the autumn return to New York, where the story itself reaches its happy-ever-after conclusion, and the novel's first draft, including doggerel inspired by the *Cautionary Tales* he had learned as a child, was complete by the spring of 1960. At the end of April, Sheila St Lawrence had read the second draft. In an enthusiastic letter full of praise for the client whose receptiveness to extravagant flattery she understood well after an association stretching back more than a decade, she congratulated Roald on having successfully made the transition from adult to children's fiction. Her letter, which pleased Roald, represented a highwater mark in a relationship that would swiftly be soured by his decision to take the handling of his foreign rights away from the Watkins Agency to his new British agents.

In hindsight, Roald's decision was a slight to St Lawrence, insensitively handled, that he may have regretted, but events in 1960 forced conventional niceties from his mind. Although Alfred Knopf acclaimed Roald's manuscript as destined to become 'a little classic', it would be many months before he was able to direct his thoughts to the forthcoming publication of his first full-length novel for children and what became, though he did not suspect it, the business of the remainder of his life.[9]

The new story on which Roald began work in 1960, a successor to *James and the Giant Peach*, would occupy him for three years and run to six drafts. As first conceived, it included detective story elements; its hero, called Charlie, as he would remain, was a 'small negro boy', whose adventures were partly a result of mistaken identity. The novel's setting was a chocolate factory, its presiding deity a quicksilver inventor whose mercurial ingenuity appealed to Roald: he would create a second similar character in a story he did not complete – Mr Billy Bubbler, 'the cleverest man in the world', who created 'Bubblers Magic Concrete Sweets' and 'Magic Hole-filling Sweets' through the wizardry of a machine Roald himself would have coveted, 'Bubblers Instant Chocolate-Making Machine', a remarkable contraption able to make chocolate from mud.[10]

Afterwards Roald described the Charlie story as he first conceived it: 'a little boy who was going round a chocolate factory and he accidentally fell into a big tub of melted chocolate and got sucked into the machine that made chocolate figures and couldn't get out'. 'I got everything wrong,' he commented.

Pat was pregnant for the third time as Roald worked on his first draft. Sexual attraction maintained a bond between the couple whose marriage had come so close to unravelling; the separations of their working lives and their sense of themselves as a family contributed a greater semblance of compatibility. In the spring they returned to

Great Missenden. From his sister Alfhild and her husband Leslie Hansen, Roald had bought a gipsy caravan that stood now in the garden: shortly he would rename Little Whitefields 'Gipsy House'. Already, though building work remained ongoing, it was at Gipsy House that Roald was happiest. In the summer of 1960, able to work in his hut in the garden, to look out – as he walked from the house to the hut – on new plantings of roses, cattle in the fields beyond and ducks on the grass, bright shoots of young spinach in the vegetable beds and, in branches in the orchard, blue and green budgerigars that roosted in a new octagonal birdhouse, his happiness appeared complete: he had restored the vanished Eden of Ty Mynedd in a corner of the Home Counties in which his mother and all three of his sisters were close at hand. What's more, he had peopled it with daughters to whom he was devoted, Olivia 'beautiful and willowy, translucent and glowing', Tessa 'sweet and chubby'; as Tessa would remember, 'his entire being was engrossed in the building of his family'.[11] Then, on 30 July, Pat gave birth to a son: Theo Matthew Roald.

Perhaps only an accident could have destroyed Roald's tranquillity so dramatically. That this happened in New York worked to complete his disillusionment with the city that, so recently, had showered him with blessings. Its victim then was four-month-old Theo.

At lunchtime, on 5 December, Susan Denson had collected Tessa from nursery school. She was pushing Theo in his pram, Tessa holding her hand, struggling too with a friend's dog. At the corner of Madison and 85th Street, when the lights changed, she stepped out into the road. The taxi that hit Theo's pram, driving too fast, accelerated rather than braking on collision. The impact hurled the pram 40 feet into the air and flung it against the side of a bus. The force crushed Theo's skull. An ambulance hastened baby, nanny and Tessa to Lenox Hill Hospital. By the time Roald and Pat arrived, Theo 'was in a state of deep shock, colourless, high pulse, temp 102 degrees'.[12] Hospital staff assumed he would die.

In its casual but devastating brutality, it was a scenario that resembled the black caprice of one of Roald's own stories. Roald, however, did not respond as a writer: emotionally or imaginatively. His response was that of Sofie Magdalene's 'Boy', a sole male accustomed to taking charge. He set aside assumptions that Theo would die to find instead means of ensuring he lived. An X-ray revealed multiple fractures to the skull but no significant internal injuries. Roald telephoned friends of Pat's, doctors Edmund Goodman and Bill Watson. By evening, four doctors were overseeing Theo's treatment. Predictably they disagreed on ways forward. Roald did not leave Theo's side. His role as arbitrator was self-appointed, characteristic of his habit of asserting control and his need for action. Ed Goodman remembered that Roald 'kept things moving'. After three days, appalled by squabbling doctors and inept nurses, but reassured by a lowering of Theo's temperature, Roald initiated a move to Ed Goodman's hospital, Columbia Presbyterian, where operations drained fluid from Theo's skull and, closely monitored, he remained for two weeks in an oxygen tent.

Uncertainty brought Roald and Pat together (Tessa's trauma would be slower to unspool: 'the devastation is beyond a small child's comprehension,' she wrote in 1988).[13] Before Christmas, Theo was released from hospital, where medical bills were already considerable, but his recovery was fraught with frightening setbacks: build-ups of cerebrospinal fluid pressing on the brain that rendered him silent, unseeing, unmoving. Every time this happened, he was hurried back to hospital for the fluid to be drained, at risk of blindness, brain damage and death. Doctors attempted to prevent further build-ups by fitting a drainage tube into his heart to enable reabsorption of the fluid. Every time the tube blocked, making another operation necessary. And each time the stakes were raised, the chances lower of restoring Theo's sight and brain function. It would continue for nine months.

The Dahls did not remain in New York. In May they made the customary crossing to Britain, Roald restless, at odds with the big, busy, dangerous city. At Gipsy House, Theo's tube blocked again. 'I couldn't believe that with everything science had come up with, they couldn't produce one little clog-proof tube,' Roald reflected; a little clog-proof tube became his mission.[14] It took two years. Although he subsequently downplayed his own part in the process, it was Roald's determination to find a non-blocking shunt to divert cerebrospinal fluid from the brain that drove development of the Wade-Dahl-Till valve afterwards manufactured and distributed globally on a not-for-profit basis. He brought together Kenneth Till, the paediatric neurosurgeon in charge of Theo at Great Ormond Street Hospital, and a toymaker from whom he had bought model aeroplanes for his nephew, Nicholas Logsdail, Else's son. Stanley Wade's particular skill was for minutely accurate metal turning. Roald labelled him 'a retired fellow with nothing much to do', a description that recalls the high-handedness with which, at school, the teenage essay-writer had addressed a pavement artist.[15] Roald involved himself closely in the two men's progress: intermediary, inspirer, inventor. Theo's own shunt would be removed for the last time in the autumn of 1963.

The process of collaboration seemed to prove to Roald

his ability to shape events by force of will, an illusion that was important to him throughout his life. Inertia and impotence frustrated him: his choice was always for action, his role, as his sister Alfhild explained, that of 'a big man, you know, a man who could cope'.[16] In the summer of 1961, as Theo made tentative steps towards recovery, Roald continued to work on the story he called *Charlie's Chocolate Boy*. Flashing lights rigged up in his writing hut alerted him to anything untoward in the nursery. Immolation in his writing offered Roald fragile escapism. With its roots in the brown cardboard boxes delivered to The Priory at Repton by Cadbury's for testing, and Roald's early dreams of inventing new tuppenny chocolate bars, his story explored disparate facets of himself. His active participation in the stages of Theo's recovery suggests a Willy Wonka role, the smilingly uncompromising magician-cum-impresario whose autonomy expressed itself in determined lawless iconoclasm, but Roald, whose life had been shaped by personal encounters, above all his friendship with Charles Marsh, had as much in common with Charlie: a home- and family-loving outsider, wide-eyed and hungry, marked by a resilient sense of wonder. Both characters share their creator's belief in magic.

The need to believe was powerful that summer. Financial reward did not motivate Roald's writing and rewriting of

Charlie's Chocolate Boy then any more than it prompted the walks in the gathering dusk on which he took Olivia and Tessa, telling them stories as night noises clustered in the trees and the fading light gave credence to fantastical tales; despite positive reviews, sales of *James and the Giant Peach* were modest. Roald distracted himself by restoring the frame of 'a very fine eighteenth-century mirror'. He took pleasure in his proficiency at the painstaking processes of water gilding. With the rigour he customarily applied to his short-lived hobbies, he had learned to water gild a decade ago at specialist framers, H. J. Spiller in Beak Street, taking detailed notes to which he referred now. 'Mr Spiller', he remembered, 'allowed me to pay his senior craftsman quite a lot of money in order to teach me for hours.'[17] At the childrens' bedtime he recited nursery rhymes, revisited his own childhood reciting Hillaire Belloc, read aloud from Beatrix Potter. Once, while they slept, he wrote Olivia and Tessa's names in weedkiller on the lawn outside their bedroom window. The following morning, he told them it was the work of fairies.

In July, Roald, Pat, Olivia, Tessa and Theo, who was well enough to learn to walk, went to Norway. They did not then return to New York. Undoubtedly Roald was the driving force behind their full-time move to Gipsy House; Olivia seconded her father's enthusiasm, drawing a picture of birds and trees and 'very tiny, in one corner ... a skyscraper and a garbage can. She wrote on it, "It's much better in England."'[18] In the spirit of amity between husband and wife that was the positive legacy of Theo's illness and their coming together over their shared fears, Pat told journalists of her happiness at living permanently in the country; it was mostly true. To a greater extent than previously, Roald's family life had taken on a settled quality: a new annexe, begun in the late spring of 1961, continued Gipsy House's transformation into the sort of home Roald had anticipated, busy with children, sisters, friends and a shifting cast of animals, including the puppy acquired a year before. On this new stage set, Pat had changed too. 'I did the cooking, I did the children, keeping the house, the garden, the weeds,' she would claim, a view others considered rosy.[19]

Yet it proved a fragile idyll. Roald's elder daughter, Olivia, died of measles on 17 November 1962. She was seven, the same age as Roald's eldest sister, Astri, whom he had been too young to remember. Like Astri's, her death was unexpected; like hers, it could have been prevented by medical intervention. A note from Olivia's preparatory school headmistress at the beginning of the month had warned of a measles outbreak; Roald and Pat's concerns were for vulnerable Theo. Measles inoculation was still uncommon, and doses of the gamma globulin antibodies to prevent it in limited supply. Pat successfully obtained serum for Theo; Olivia caught measles and, in isolation from her siblings, the illness ran its course. Roald taught her to play chess; he teased her for her 'polka dots'.[20] 'I can remember reading to her often in bed and not feeling particularly alarmed about it,' he wrote long afterwards.

> Then one morning, when she was well on the road to recovery, I was sitting on her bed showing her how to fashion little animals out of coloured pipe-cleaners, and when it came to her turn to make one herself, I noticed that her fingers and her mind were not working together and she couldn't do anything. 'Are you feeling all right?', I asked her. 'I feel all sleepy,' she said. In an hour, she was unconscious. In twelve hours she was dead.[21]

She had contracted an inflammation of the brain called measles encephalitis, an outcome unlikely with the preventative of gamma globulin.

Four decades earlier, Harald Dahl had died in the wake of his favourite daughter's death. Roald's was a death of the heart, its imprint indelible. In a story he had written in 1944 about a mother contemplating the death of her fighter pilot son, he allowed her the bleakest conclusion: 'If something did happen, then you too would be dead.'[22] In November

1962, Roald had yet to recover from the strain of Theo's long illness: in the wake of Olivia's death, what Pat described as an 'avalanche of anger and frustration' expressed itself in silence.[23] Roald said nothing: withdrawn, hermetic, lost. He turned to his mother, who had suffered similarly, but not Pat, whose grief matched his own; no longer bound to Pat by the shared anxieties of Theo's accident, he railed at her tentative conviction of a reunion with Olivia in an afterlife. He shielded none of his family from the force of his wordless sorrow. For years he had taken painkillers for his back; now he increased his dose, again he began drinking heavily. The result, wrote Tessa, was a family that 'toppled unwittingly over the edge of a jagged cliff face into a canyon of darkness which was filled with such sadness, such total devastation that we would never recover'.[24]

Roald divided his time between his writing hut, where nothing came between him and the magnitude of his suffering, and the garden he laid out around Olivia's grave beside the church in neighbouring Little Missenden where all three children had been christened. In a green-covered exercise book, he wrote a terse account of the final hospital dash and Olivia's death – 'I kissed her. She was still warm. I went out' – then firmly he hid the book from sight, its existence unknown to his family until his own death, and he hung up a painting of Olivia, which remained in place, visible from his writing chair, through three decades.[25] Like the painting, to which, in this way, Pat was denied access, Olivia's garden was a focus of private communing. A morbid grandeur characterized its conception. Roald took advice from one of the country's foremost experts in alpine plants, Valerie Finnis, afterwards a recipient of the Royal Horticultural Society's prestigious Royal Victoria Medal. Finnis, based nearby in Oxfordshire, advised on the garden's 200 plants. That creation and maintenance were labour-intensive suited Roald's purpose. Roald claimed he 'was in a kind of daze': at Pat's suggestion, he contacted his former headmaster, Geoffrey Fisher, who, the previous year, had retired as Archbishop of Canterbury, but though he thanked Fisher for his help and sent him copies of two of his collections of stories, Roald derived little comfort from their meeting and none of the certainties he had sought concerning eternal life.[26] There had always been a gossamer quality to his religious faith: with Olivia's death, his doubts coalesced into non-belief. Over time, a creed of his own, rooted in kindness and respect for the natural world, alongside a truculently child-like sense of wonder, sustained him: the doctrine of good thoughts versus ugly thoughts that he expounded in *The Twits*. But not yet. To friends Pat lamented the solitariness of Roald's working life, which provided no distractions from his sorrow. Roald applied himself to understanding the exact nature of Olivia's susceptibility, on the surface a facts-based, coolly rational reaction akin to his response to the problem of Theo's shunt. The swiftness of her death had debarred him from action to safeguard her: retrospectively – fruitlessly – he struggled to fill the gaps in his knowledge, certain of a connection between measles encephalitis and Olivia's repeated non-reaction to smallpox vaccinations that would explain and make sense of what had happened. His correspondence with leading specialists lasted as long as his grief. Perhaps he meant to make amends through investigations likely to benefit others; perhaps a sense of guilt – undeserved but powerful – demanded slaking by reassurance that nothing could have been foretold.

'My daughter was congenitally immune to smallpox (no vaccination ever took) and being immune to smallpox she was susceptible to encephalitis,' Roald wrote to Dr John Adams of the department of paediatrics at the University of California in 1966. 'Has anyone checked up the smallpox vaccination history of recent cases of encephalitis ...? There is a clue here, I'm certain of it.'[27]

For more than twenty years Roald's letters pursued the missing clue, 'like a blind man who looks towards something but does not see', but no answers lessened his grief.[28] Even in his own last illness, contemplation of Olivia's death left him wordless.

Roald's sadness plays no part in the novel whose title he had changed that summer to *Charlie and the Chocolate Factory*. Joyfully, the adventure prefigured in his ideas book as 'a chocolate factory that makes fantastic and marvellous things – and a crazy man running it' celebrated his lifelong love of chocolate and the boundless ingenuity of its imperious wizard inventor.[29] The novel rewards good behaviour and, in Charlie's selection as Willy Wonka's heir, holds out a promise for the future. When it was finished, Roald accepted what he called a 'monstrous bribe': 'A big New York publisher had the idea of asking a selected number of the so-called best novelists writing in the English language each to write for them a short children's book, and a large enough advance was offered to tempt most of the candidates into having a go.'[30] Roald's own go became *The Magic Finger*, originally called *The Almost Ducks*, completed in the bleakness of a winter in which everything numbed him save the quickness of his grief. For the first time his heroine is a girl: she is the age Olivia would have been at the book's completion. The story's protest against shooting would shape Roald's later novel, *Danny the Champion of the World*. 'I have yet to be convinced that a man has the right to kill the anopheles mosquito merely because his strength and brains enable him to do so, or to kill any other animal, reptile or insect,' Roald wrote in his ideas book. 'Obviously it is murder.'[31] Like other authors' offerings in an ill-fated project, *The Magic Finger* foundered, rights reverted back to Roald, and the book was not published until 1966. Five years after he had begun work on *James and the Giant Peach*, Roald still had only one children's novel in print, and no interest from British publishers. Nor had he published a single story for adult readers during the same period. In a plaintive letter to Alfred Knopf, he resorted to oenophile imagery: the bottle of short story inspiration, he wrote, now contained only sediment.[32]

Under these circumstances, it was inevitable that, in April 1964, reporting on the plan by Great Missenden Parish Council to oppose Roald's application to transform a garage in the village into an antiques shop to raise funds for a children's charity, the *Buckinghamshire Examiner* should describe him again as the 'husband of actress Patricia Neal'.[33] Roald could not protest: weeks before, Pat had been nominated for an Oscar as Best Actress for a film called *Hud*, shot in Texas in June 1962. Days later, eight months pregnant and asleep in the early hours of the morning, she learned by telephone that she had won. At Roald's suggestion, his old flame Annabella accepted the award on Pat's behalf. Despite the lingering trauma of Olivia's death, it was a moment of straightforward happiness for Pat, consolidated the following month with the birth of her fourth child, a daughter whom the Dahls called Ophelia, like Olivia a Shakespearean name. Roald's own good news lacked the public acclaim of Pat's Academy Awards success, which he envied her. In January, he had rejected an offer of a quick settlement on the part of film giant MGM. Both he and Pat believed the studio's script for a film called *36 Hours* plagiarized one of Roald's wartime short stories. Roald was determined MGM would pay for its theft and refused to accept less than $25,000. 'It is not often in a lifetime that a storywriter has a full movie based on his story,' he wrote to Mike Watkins, his agent since Sheila St Lawrence's departure to live in Ireland with her family.[34] Watkins wavered, but as so often in his literary dealings, Roald had no intention of capitulating. His obduracy paid off: in April, MGM transferred $30,000 into a bank account for Roald's children. This sum comfortably exceeded his current earnings from his children's fiction, which he described, in a statement he would later be forced to rescind, as 'an uneconomic diversion'.[35] Publication of *Charlie and the Chocolate Factory* by Knopf in October, however, offered a tentative foretaste of things to come:

within a month, an initial print run of 10,000 copies had sold out. Closer to home, Hamish Hamilton turned down the book. Chatto & Windus reached the same decision months later. 'I refuse to be rejected right and left,' a peevish Roald had told his British agent Laurence Pollinger with customary imperiousness, but he was in no position to lay down conditions.[36]

For Roald, the crisis in his professional life persisted even as Pat's star continued to rise. He denied any element of commercial compromise in a story of voyeuristic titillation, 'The Visitor', which the men's magazine *Playboy* accepted for publication early in 1965, following its rejection by the *New Yorker*. To a request for his photograph from the magazine's fiction editor Ray Russell, Roald responded good-humouredly: 'Having seen some of the astonishing photographs in your magazine lately, I am ashamed to be able only to send you this ordinary thing. If there had been time I'd have had one taken emerging like Brunhilde from my bath amid clouds of steam with nothing but a loofa to hide my privates.'[37] In his flippancy was no trace of foreboding.

Disaster, when it struck, was instant and unexpected: its reverberations would impact on Roald's family even beyond his death. The victim on this occasion was Pat. It happened in Los Angeles, in mid-February 1965, four days into filming a new picture by John Ford called *Seven Women*. Pat was three months pregnant, a secret shared only with Roald. Neither she nor her unborn baby died, but it was Pat, not the baby, who would require nursing for weeks and months and years to come.

VIII

CRITICAL
CONDITION
1965–1971

'I must not let them down.'

THE BULLETIN ISSUED to the press on 20 February gave few grounds for hope. 'Miss Neal has not regained consciousness. Since surgery there has been no noticeable change, either good or bad.'[1] An update three days later suggested stasis: Pat, said the hospital spokesman, was 'still in a critical condition'.[2] Back in Britain, the *Daily Mirror* tugged at the heart strings: 'The Oscar-winning actress whose home life has been marred by tragedy is near death herself.'[3]

In a borrowed house in Hollywood, bathing Tessa in the early evening, Pat had experienced searing pains in her left temple. She called for Roald, who suspected a stroke. Roald made a series of telephone calls, all to the same number, successful at the third attempt. Within ten minutes husband and wife were in an ambulance, Pat on oxygen, heading for UCLA Medical Center. Left behind with their new Scottish nanny Sheena Burt, Theo was disorientated and Tessa, still naked and warm from the bath, desolate, hearing sirens wailing for the third time in her short life.

At a crisis of faith, Roald had arranged a meeting with the former Archbishop of Canterbury. Intrigued by water gilding, he had visited the country's leading specialist to find out more. He wrote a story about a bet between wine buffs: 'I was in London when I wrote it and I got hold of the address of the most celebrated wine man in the world at the time, André Simon, and I simply went to his house and rang the bell and asked if he would be good enough to read my story and check the facts.'[4] In a Los Angeles bedroom, alarmed when his wife lost consciousness, Roald had done as he always did: he asked for help from the most eminent specialist he knew, in this case neurosurgeon Charles Carton.

Carton was waiting at the hospital when the Dahls' ambulance arrived. After two and a half hours of X-rays, he examined the pictures' evidence of subarachnoid haemorrhage caused by a ruptured aneurysm, a weakness in the wall of a blood vessel – 'a small dot, the size of a farthing, over the left temporal lobe', as it appeared to Roald staring at the large, wet photographs on the viewing screens.[5] Then he operated, beginning at midnight. In a seven-hour procedure Carton removed blood clots from Pat's brain, clipped the aneurysm to prevent further rupture and reinforced the artery wall. He had told Roald that without the operation Pat would die; he suggested she would almost certainly not survive surgery either; and, with the operation over, he worried that she would suffer severe mental and physical disabilities. Throughout the endless night Roald remained in the hospital, battling the Nordic fatalism he had inherited from Sofie Magdalene, sceptical about superstition but unable to pray and determined, he suggested later, not to succumb to self-pity: Theo ... Olivia ... and now Pat.

Ten days later, Pat was still unconscious. Roald wrote to his mother, offering her a diligent account of everything that had happened since 17 February. His version is brisk but compassionate, and Roald did not downplay his own role: 'I called in Dr Carton … The X-raying took two-and-a-half hours. When I was called in to inspect the pictures, it was about 10.30 p.m. … I said, "What will happen if you don't operate?" He said, "Then she will die for certain." So I said, "You must operate at once." He agreed.'[6] Roald likened what followed to a waiting game, the visits to Pat's bedside that began at 6.30 each morning and continued on and off daylong, until his return to the house in Pacific Palisades at eleven o'clock at night. To his mother he pointed out reasons for optimism – 'The left side is okay. The face is unaffected and looks normal … She's getting fantastic attention, and every possible medical aid'; he itemized concerns: aside from Pat's own prospects, Tessa's unsettlement. Of course, he did not mention his own response. 'The key thing,' he decided, 'was not to get depressed and feel sorry for yourself. You had to rise to the challenge. Do something. Anything was better than nothing.'[7]

It was an expression of his sincerest belief. Doing something had saved Theo, while the impossibility of action in Olivia's case would haunt him until death. In the operation's immediate aftermath, doing consisted of a bedside vigil he broke only to eat and sleep, undeterred by his wife's unrecognizability (bandage-swathed, hairless, attached to drips and tubes, motionless, silent, eyes closed in impenetrable sleep), Roald repeating and repeating and repeating, 'Pat, this is Roald', his only respite frequent self-affirming visits to the children's department of a bookshop opposite the hospital: 'when his wife was recuperating at the UCLA Medical Center,' the shop's owner told fellow children's author P. L. Travers, he 'kept us supplied with autographed copies of *Charlie and the Chocolate Factory*.'[8] When it came, in the third week, Pat's response was electrifying, first a squeeze of his hand, then a flickering open of her right eye; days later she opened both eyes. She could say nothing; instead she smiled: she was going to live. Roald had been sure of this outcome, or determined to be sure, despite doctors' forebodings, a feeling Pat would claim she shared: 'I remember seeing them looking down at me and thinking, "My heart beat won't stop. It just won't stop."'[9] Afterwards Roald acknowledged no sense of elation. 'I saw the slow, mysterious recovery of a brain that had been severely insulted,' he remembered, 'and the steady return to consciousness of the owner of that brain', a detached-sounding observation, like the narratives of his short stories, with their cool chronologies of ill fortune and mischance.[10]

Then one day Pat, like Roald a smoker, reached out a hand for Roald's cigarette, and he allowed himself to smile. A nurse sang as she worked. Falteringly, hazarding a single note, Pat joined in. She tried to speak, but names and words were lost to her.

Ed Goodman described the spectacle of the Oscar-winning actress, ravaged and almost destroyed, as 'pitiful'.[11] Roald's refusal – on the surface at least – to permit himself pity for his vegetative wife divided the couple's friends. That Pat should recover and recover fully became Roald's obsessive concern: once again, as Tessa remembered, he had engrossed himself entirely in engineering by whatever means possible the miraculous turnaround needed to preserve his family. More than any doctor, nurse or therapist, Roald dominated the hesitant steps of Pat's recovery. That she would live, get better, walk, talk, think, act again became articles of faith for him, however long the odds. As a storyteller he would encourage generations of children, including his own children, to believe in magic; in a hospital room in Los Angeles, amid the pink marble luxury of a Hollywood mansion and at home in Gipsy House, Roald also believed. In these tense, slow, repetitive days, two battles surged: Pat's struggle to return to life and the battle Roald fought within himself to bring about the impossible apparently through force of will.

'Everyone is very braced by Pat's condition,' Roald told Sofie Magdalene when, after little more than a month, she was released from hospital, her right leg in a steel brace, a patch over her left eye to screen her double vision.[12] He exaggerated. The horror Tessa had experienced, taken by Roald with Theo to see her mother in hospital after Pat came round, could not be shaken off: Roald had miscalculated in assuming that their reunion at the earliest opportunity would benefit them all, adding to Tessa's suffering. Pat herself was far from braced: she was angry, struggling and, frequently, bored; she was prey to depression and agonies of self-pity, and drained physically and emotionally by her pregnancy. Roald was exhausted – at times carrying Pat up and down stairs – but exhilarated by his sense of purpose. When she was well enough to take stock, Pat succumbed to resentment, too. Encouraged by Charles Marsh, she had long ago forfeited any claim to dominance in her marriage, but the shared crises of Theo's accident and Olivia's death had shown both Pat and Roald the possibility of a less fractious togetherness. In the altered reality of her new life, Roald now her browbeating Pygmalion, was no pretence of parity between spouses.

To cheat death was not enough for Roald: he was determined that Pat would relearn to be herself. Charles Carton advised that her therapy begin as soon as possible on leaving hospital and, with customary thoroughness, Roald hired a nurse, a physiotherapist and a speech therapist (the expense of this arrangement would shortly provoke troubled references to 'this vast household').[13] He overruled suggestions that to attempt more than an hour's rehabilitation a day would overtax Pat and even prove counterproductive: the programme of mental and physical stimulation he put in place occupied much of her day, often to her intense frustration, sharpened by fear and tiredness. The regime was punishing, characterized by Roald's apparent certainty of success and an attitude that upset some of Pat's many visitors: encouragement but not sympathy and a consistent denial of grounds for self-pity. Roald's aim was to shield Pat from 'inertia, boredom, frustration and depression'; he had decided that 'very drastic action would have to be taken' if Pat were to avoid becoming 'a bad-tempered desperately unhappy nitwit'.[14] In 1960s Hollywood, this pre-war British mindset jarred. One friend described Roald as fierce and unrelenting; his programme for Pat's improvement, she decided, resembled 'the way one trains a dog'.[15] The views of others more closely involved differed. Sheena Burt wrote to Sofie Magdalene that Roald was 'such a strong man one feels one can carry on with his inspiration and guidance'.[16] It was the part that for so long Roald had played for his mother and sisters, the part he allotted himself, Sheena's his desired response, the equivalent of Mrs Fox's refrain-like acclamation of Mr Fox as 'a fantastic fox'.[17]

By late spring, Pat was well enough to travel and, on 17 May, the Dahls returned to Gipsy House. Like Pat, the house had altered dramatically in their absence. A magazine makeover had changed doors and floors; dark-brown walls and carpet in the drawing room had horrified Sofie Magdalene as work proceeded and appalled Roald too. Returning the house to its pre-makeover state – eliminating 'the colour of elephant turds'[18] – offered him distraction from Pat's treatment, which Roald entrusted to a roster of volunteers, mainly friends and neighbours. They kept Pat busy with stories read aloud, word and memory games, 'like a kindergarten child, reading, writing and arithmetic', as if, Tessa remembered, her mother 'was miraculously growing up at the same speed as me. I was nine, and so was she.'[19] His own role at Gipsy House Roald described as 'running the house ... earning a living and above all, keeping cheerful'.[20] As in Los Angeles, visitors reached their own conclusions. Roald's cheerfulness had a brittle quality – an act of will, it sometimes seemed, rather than genuine optimism, and Pat was frequently in tears or withdrawn or truculent or abusive. She threatened suicide. She called her husband 'Roald the Rotten' and, at other times, 'Roald the Bastard' and a slave driver; in the autobiography she wrote in 1988, after the Dahls' divorce, she admitted that she had hated his coaxing and cudgelling. Roald referred to his efficiency and busyness: 'I'm frightfully good at blocking off one side,' he told Valerie Eaton Griffith, who had become Pat's chief therapist.[21] The efficiency he referred to concerned his wife's recovery from a near-death experience and the side he blocked off was his emotional engagement with this process. Pat felt herself powerless to affect his behaviour beyond angering or disappointing him. Speech continued to trouble her. At first, she could remember only a handful of words, resorting to idiosyncratic neologisms that Roald (in this case 'Roald the writer') noted carefully and recycled later. Like the BFG, Pat knew, or thought she knew, 'what words I am wanting to say, but somehow or other they is always getting squiff squiddled around … what I mean and what I says is two different things'.[22] Roald forced Pat to work hard to find the right words, as he forced her to practise exercises aimed at restoring full use to her limbs, and discouraged friends from helping her in and out of cars, up and down stairs or steps. 'A hundred per cent recovery' remained his stubborn mantra: one visitor referred to a 'need for perfection … so extreme that I was very glad I was not … anyone close to him'.[23] 'He had me working from when I woke up in the morning until I went to bed at night,'

Pat remembered. Years later, she changed her mind about Roald's hectoring: 'He really did do a wondrous job,' she told an interviewer in 1996. 'He was a very good man.'[24]

Pat's baby was born in the first week of August, the Dahls' fifth and last child, a daughter called Lucy. Roald gave Pat a ring he had bought at Sotheby's, a classical intaglio carved with an image of Persephone, the goddess associated with spring, nature's yearly return to life. Photographs of mother and new baby appeared in many newspapers. Readers were reminded that Pat was married to Roald; on this occasion, he was described as a screenwriter.

His work was on Roald's mind. Six months earlier, he had envied Pat's success. Now, though he spoke publicly about her return to acting, it was clear that, in the short term, her ability to generate her former income had evaporated. Despite medical insurance, Pat's US hospital bills were considerable; the nurse, physiotherapist and speech therapist Roald had employed in Los Angeles had added to his expenses. In a letter of thanks written on Pat's behalf for flowers sent at Lucy's birth, Roald briefly let down his guard. 'Life is a bit of a struggle, isn't it?' he asked rhetorically.[25] Not, however, for much longer. Weeks before, Roald had received $67,500 from United Artists for a screenplay, *Oh Death, Where Is Thy Sting-a-ling-a-ling?*, that he had written in the summer of 1964, after

meeting a young director called Robert Altman. Altman
had suggested to Roald a story after his own heart: a raid
by First World War fighter pilots on a Zeppelin base on
the German/Swiss border. Roald's acceptance was casual
and good-humoured: he and Altman made a rights-
sharing agreement, based on Altman selling the film to a
studio with himself as director. But the offer of $150,000
made by United Artists early in 1965 explicitly excluded
Altman. Angrily the younger man turned it down, and
Roald's promise of $75,000 vanished. That Roald would
have behaved in the same way in Altman's position did
not temper the fury of his reaction at a moment when
Pat's illness was already straining his resources. With the
vigour he always reserved for financial dealings, Roald
employed bigshot Hollywood agent Swifty Lazar to fight
his corner, and Altman gave in. In the autumn, Roald
received a second payment from United Artists – this
time for $25,000 – for rewriting the script in line with its
new director's requirements, though, like *The Gremlins*, the
project would be abandoned over the course of the year.
Screened in October, a BBC2 dramatization of 'Parson's
Pleasure', one of the stories in *Kiss Kiss*, adapted by Philip
Levene, writer of a new series of *The Avengers*, was less
lucrative for Roald, but helped restore his confidence at
a time when he was struggling to find material for adult

stories, and indeed markets for the few stories he did complete.

Only *Playboy*, it seemed, kept faith with him, and then strictly on its own terms. After 'The Visitor', in January 1966 the magazine published 'The Last Act', which the *New Yorker* had turned down on grounds of its unpleasantness (Roald described its troubling plot as 'murder by fucking'); the alterations it made to the story, without consulting Roald, predictably enraged him. Nevertheless, the following year, Roald accepted from *Playboy* a commission for one of his rare journalistic forays. '007's Oriental Eyefuls' is an arch exercise in blokeishness that begins with a conversation between Pat and Roald at Gipsy House:

'"A man called Broccoli wants you on the telephone," Pat said.

'I had never in my life heard of anyone with a name like that. "It's Archie Lockley," I said. "Lockley. Try to say it properly." She still had occasional trouble with names.'

This exchange is entirely imaginary, and Roald knew well who Albert 'Cubby' Broccoli was when, in 1966, Broccoli and Harry Saltzman, producer-owners of the James Bond film franchise, approached him to write the screenplay for the fifth Bond film, *You Only Live Twice*. It was the final twist to the happy ending of Roald's unhappy fallout with Robert Altman over *Oh Death, Where Is Thy Sting-a-ling-a-ling?*

– Saltzman and Broccoli had seen and admired Roald's *Sting-a-ling* script – and it proved a turning point in Roald's life. Payments for his script totalling $165,500 (equivalent today to around $1.5 million) completed the reversal in Roald and Pat's professional fortunes set in motion by Pat's stroke. From now on, Roald not Pat would provide for their family financially, just as Roald not Pat had taken on the primary carer's role towards their four children. For so long on a stop-start trajectory, the financial side of Roald's career would never seriously falter again. Yet this change of direction, in so many ways serendipitous, was not of his own choosing. Roald's 'only real ambition', he told Alfred Knopf, perhaps to save face, was to produce a new collection of stories for adult readers; he decried the Bond commission as distasteful.[26] Save in *Playboy*, where he enthused 'the reason [Bond is] so good, so much better than all the other comic-strip men of action we see around us is that he's thoroughly believable', in public he maintained this lofty detachment towards the project (in private, his enjoyment was evident: to his children he offered daily updates on Bond's progress as he wrote; the side of Roald that had revelled in millionaires' lifestyles in Washington enjoyed the project's extravagance, including the Rolls-Royce sent to Gipsy House to collect script updates and transport them at speed to London). In a letter to Blanche Campbell, owner of a Los Angeles bookshop, Roald referred on completion to 'my silly James Bond film'.[27] Unable to prevent himself from boasting even in the act of denigration, he reminded her of the film's forthcoming royal premiere.

Roald's view of the weakness of Fleming's plot was widely shared, including by Saltzman and Broccoli: 'It's all rather a muddle and scarcely in the tradition of Secret Service fiction,' Malcolm Muggeridge had written, and Roald would claim he used 'only four or five' of the original story's ideas.[28] As shot, the film wanders a long way from the novel. How many of its innovations were actually Roald's is unclear. Roald certainly had access to suggestions made by an Oscar-nominated screenwriter previously consulted by the producers: Harold Jack Bloom claimed that the film was in fact his work. Roald was happy to take the credit. The film's fantastical elements and ironic self-parody suggest his imagination and his mischief, and his Bond shares his own taste for caviar. Key to Roald's larger enjoyment, however, given his fiercely protective attitude to his work, was his conviction that director Lewis Gilbert had refrained from any changes to his script. He fared less well the following year, when Broccoli persuaded him to take on a second Fleming project: adapting the Bond author's children's novel, *Chitty Chitty Bang Bang*. For Roald, for whom the financial incentive was potent, the experience proved 'ghastly', marred by acrimonious exchanges with director Ken Hughes and his own lack of any real engagement. 'Once you get a rotten director, or an egocentric director, you're dead,' Roald reflected in 1983, apportioning blame squarely, as was his wont.[29] Hughes rewrote much of Roald's script, ultimately claiming it as all his own work, much as Roald had sidelined Harold Jack Bloom. The experience soured Roald's relationship with Broccoli; it hardened the dislike of the film industry he had nurtured since the collapse of Disney's Gremlins project. 'They pay a lot, so you take the money and run,' Roald said later. Like *You Only Live Twice*, much in *Chitty Chitty Bang Bang* had no origin in Fleming's story. If Hughes's claims to authorship are correct, retrospective criticism of Roald on grounds of anti-Semitism in the characterization of the Child Catcher, the film's villain who is not present in the novel – part of a wider criticism, which emerged later, of Roald's anti-Semitism – appears unfounded.

Roald's disillusionment with film-making was clear in a letter he sent Blanche Campbell early the following year. He was still recovering from a protracted hospital stay in November, as a result of worsening back pain and, with good reason, feeling self-pity of the sort he had so ruthlessly denied Pat. An operation to remove pieces of vertebral bone in order to relieve agonizing pressure on his spinal cord had failed to heal; in its wake emerged bowel problems that revealed a fistula in the lower colon, which necessitated a second operation. In the middle of the crisis, unanticipated by Roald, Sofie Magdalene died at the age of eighty-two, on the fifth anniversary of Olivia's death. Too ill to attend her funeral, Roald was well enough to understand the extent of his devastation at the loss of the woman who, more than Pat, had remained his emotional buoy. 'I've been having a rough time,' he wrote with characteristic understatement.

Just got out of hospital. Two spinal operations for a massive disc that paralyzed the left leg. Much better now and I'm beginning to walk again and to get back into shape. One good thing – it stopped me writing movie scripts. When I start again, I'm going to try to do either stories or another children's book. *Charlie [and the Chocolate Factory]* & *James [and the Giant Peach]* were published in England 4 weeks before Christmas. Both have been the juvenile best sellers since then. Charlie has sold 12,000 in 3 weeks, and James about 8,000. I must try to write another – if only I can gather the energy.[30]

Among his mother's effects was a very large cactus that Roald placed in the greenhouse in which he kept his collection of orchids, another of the private enclosed spaces he had craved from boyhood. About this offbeat memento was a curious poignancy.

As so often, Roald was energized by success – not, in this instance, the commercial success of both recent films but belated publication in the UK of his two full-length children's books. Again, serendipity played its part: the father of one of Tessa's school friends had noted her absorption in a book that turned out to be an American edition of *James and the Giant Peach*. The father in question, Rayner Unwin, was the major shareholder in the publishing company George Allen & Unwin and a near neighbour in Little Missenden. Although aware of Roald's well-deserved reputation for being difficult, Unwin agreed to issue *James and the Giant Peach* and *Charlie and the Chocolate Factory* in November 1967 in an unorthodox deal of Roald's making that would subsequently make him very rich indeed: in place of the usual advance-then-royalties contract, the publishing house promised Roald 50 per cent of all receipts. *The Magic Finger* would shortly follow. Meanwhile, in the States, Knopf's accounts department calculated that, from sales of *James* and *Charlie*, Roald was owed almost $1 million; there were also much smaller payments due for *Kiss Kiss* and *Someone Like You*. Fan letters from American children, to all of which Roald tried to reply, arrived at a rate of more than fifty a week. No longer would the novels' irascible author be able to describe juvenile fiction as 'uneconomic'. At Gipsy House, Roald built a swimming pool: it was another of the markers of success by which he set such store. Increasingly concerned to safeguard his income from the Inland Revenue, he began to evolve a scheme by which Knopf would pay him a proportion of his US royalties in the form of a modest income, while the remainder accrued on account. In doing so, he set a time bomb ticking.

The element of self-congratulation that came to colour his next novel, *Fantastic Mr Fox*, had been earned in a remorseless decade, and it was no coincidence that Roald chose this moment to embark on a story about a family successfully fighting for its very survival. In the Foxes' life-and-death struggle with Boggis, Bunce and Bean, set under a beech tree at the top of the Gipsy House orchard, victory emerges from Mr Fox's resourcefulness and generosity and the family's willingness to pull together. 'What fine children I have, [Mr Fox] thought. They are starving to death and they haven't had a drink for three days, but they are still undefeated. I must not let them down.'[31] Mourning Sofie Magdalene, still devastated by Olivia's death and physically battered, Roald at last felt able to confront the future with less belligerent confidence. 'The outside is full of enemies ... but now, my friends, we have an entirely new set-up,' announces Mr Fox at the story's close. There is much cheering and, from Mrs Fox, a simple statement of admiration and gratitude: 'MY HUSBAND IS A FANTASTIC FOX.'[32] Earlier in the novel she has already said something similar. On that occasion, in a response worthy of Roald himself, 'Mr Fox looked at his wife and smiled. He loved her more than ever when she said things like that.'[33]

Like most self-fictions, *Fantastic Mr Fox* contained its measure of wishful thinking. Pat had never conformed to Mrs Fox's pipe-and-slippers-fetching 'little woman' model of wifehood and, like their mother, Roald's 'fine' children, especially Tessa, were less biddable than the little Foxes. Tessa's predictable unhappiness was of long duration, beginning with the trauma of Theo's accident. A year after the accident, Roald had taken Tessa to leading child psychoanalyst Anna Freud, but he resisted Freud's advice of family therapy: none of his friends, he claimed in Tessa's account written after his death, could ever write again 'after they had had all their nooks and crannies flattened like pancakes'.[34] Untreated, compounded by the horrors of Olivia's death and Pat's strokes, Tessa's traumas made her exacting and miserable, but Roald was as reluctant to discuss his daughter's unhappiness with her as he was to talk about his own feelings, incapable then, as always, of responding to suggestions of emotional neediness.

He was also preoccupied by his relationship with Pat.

Within a year of Pat's accident, Roald was wrestling with his marriage's future. Pat was not a different person from the woman Roald had married. Rather she had become an exaggerated version of her former self, and the traits that were magnified were those that appealed least to Roald: her narcissism, which Tessa has claimed her parents shared, self-indulgence, strident anger – 'I can't calm down,' Pat told the *New York Post* in 1973 – lack of intellectual interests and theatrical qualities dismissed as 'actressy'; she herself claimed she had lost any sense of nervousness, the ability to consider abstractions or to dream.[35] Again Roald took advice from Geoffrey Fisher that, as before, apparently offered meagre solace. Roald's feelings were uncomfortably conflicted. 'I love her,' he wrote to a close friend about Pat, 'I'll never leave her. But I have to live with her all the time, and you would go round the bend within a couple of hours.'[36] It was a dispiriting prospect and almost certainly unworkable.

Confused, Roald misjudged a project that may have been intended to unite husband and wife. He set out to make his own vehicle for Pat, bought rights to a first novel, embarked on the screenplay, found a producer and a director and made a deal with a production company linked to MGM. Roald boasted that his adaptation of *Nest in a Falling Tree* was his best to date; he had added to the heroine's back story by making her, like Pat, a former stroke victim. Joy Cowley's novel was tense, even chilling. In Roald's hands, it acquired some of the hallmarks of his short stories: dollops of melodrama, a preoccupation with sex, flashes of humour. The results were uneven, despite the quality of Pat's performance. Not for the first or last time, Roald blamed everyone and everything else. Pat derived little pleasure from the experience: she was convinced she overheard director Alistair Reid maligning her. Roald described Reid as a 'very nasty little man'; to Roald's first biographer, Jeremy Treglown, Reid described Roald as 'a bully, a big, overpoweringly enormous guy. He would make [Pat] repeat things in front of people, and treat her like a child.'[37] Released in the States as *The Night Digger* in May 1971, the film garnered poor reviews; it was not released in Britain.

Did Pat reflect on the story Roald had chosen for them to tell together? Cowley's novel is a claustrophobic account of a spinster daughter compelled to care for her demanding invalid mother. Roald appeared unaware of grounds for discomfort on Pat's part. Pat would argue that she had already glimpsed the precariousness of her marriage.

IX

SUCH DAZZLING
LOVELINESS
1971–1983

'The joys of this world belong to the fighters.'

I N *THE NIGHT DIGGER*, Pat's character Maura Prince, her mother's beleaguered carer, allows herself to fall in love with an outsider who offers her distractions. Something similar happened to Roald.

That year, in an interview for the *National Enquirer*, Pat described her life as 'good. It's really beautiful – even though the producers aren't chasing me anymore'.[1] For the time being, she did not lament this professional hiatus. 'I like living in the country and being a housewife, and cooking and washing, then going off to work when something good comes along,' she told an Australian journalist.[2] As she also admitted, she liked money. In 1972, she agreed to make a series of short advertisements for Maxim instant coffee. The stylist in charge of her wardrobe would become Pat's friend, her husband's mistress and, after a decade, replace Pat as Roald's wife.

Roald had recently completed *Charlie and the Great Glass Elevator*, a sequel to *Charlie and the Chocolate Factory* prompted by the novel's continuing popularity. On 17 October 1971, he told Blanche Campbell, 'I am trying at last, as a result of a good deal of pressure from kids, to do a sequel to 'Charlie'. So far it's coming out a bit odd, but that doesn't worry me. What does worry me is where the hell we go when I finish the next chapter'.[3] Roald may have hoped that the act of writing a sequel would mitigate his unhappiness at the recent film musical based on the earlier book. 'The film of Charlie was pretty poor, wasn't it?' he wrote to Campbell. It was Roald's last venture into writing for films. He had written the screenplay himself, but as always jibbed at his lack of control over the film-making process. 'I really am appalled by the petty tinkering with lines all through the screenplay without consideration,' he wrote to producer Robert Newman.

> One tiny example – page 10. Turkentine's speeches have been rewritten and the operative word 'nitro-glycerin' has been left out. That's the whole point. And what on earth is the point of the new long speech by Turkentine at the bottom of p. 10???? Pure bullshit. I am really very much cut-up about the whole way these rewrites have been handled.[4]

Afterwards he reacted less angrily to suggestions that he 'tinker' with passages of the novel itself dealing with the Oompa-Loompas. Sectors of American opinion were increasingly vocal in categorizing Roald's 'African Pygmies' as racist. Seldom averse to notoriety in his public life and, in his private life, happy to shock, frequently to the point of giving lasting offence to those on the receiving end of his verbal coruscations, usually at the supper table after too much to drink, Roald was clear that he did not mean to upset his child readers. A new edition of the novel transformed the Oompa-Loompas, investing them with 'rosy-white' skin and long 'golden brown' hair; new illustrations reflected these changes.[5] To Roald's distress, film-makers had used dwarves in *Willy Wonka and the Chocolate Factory*: 'Those ghastly Oompa-Loompas – seven dirty old dwarfs – were horrible. I get nightmares about them,' he told Blanche Campbell. He excluded Oompa-Loompas from *Charlie and the Great Glass Elevator*.

In Roald and Pat's lives appeared a young woman of winning charm, Felicity Crosland, known as 'Liccy' (pronounced 'Lissy'). Roald was fifty-six, but looked older, still troubled by his back, limping as he walked – he would toy with a theory that large men wore out sooner than their shorter counterparts. Two decades earlier, he may have regretted his hair loss: in his ideas books are suggestions for stories about hair restoration – 'A fellow really did discover by chance a substance that made a thick growth of hair appear suddenly on his bald head.'[6] To the young woman, he retained a twinkle in his eye, considerable energy and a forceful presence. For her part, from her Indian father and English mother (in a detail Roald appreciated, a member of an old Catholic gentry family), she inherited striking and unusual good looks. His effect on her, like hers on him, was instantaneous and overwhelming. Roald fell in love on the spot, like Oswald's first encounter with Yasmin Howcomely in the novel he wrote at a midpoint in their affair, *My Uncle Oswald*, Yasmin 'a creature of such dazzling loveliness' that Oswald 'gap[es] and goggl[es] at her as though she were Cleopatra herself reincarnated'.[7] In her mid-thirties, Liccy was separated from her husband, with whom her three daughters, aged twelve, eleven and ten, lived. She was not literary, but nor was Roald, who did not discuss his writing with his family and mostly avoided the company of other writers. Absorbed from Sofie Magdalene, Roald's interests were those Tessa identified as central to civilized marriage in her novel *Working for Love*: 'paintings, furniture, music or wine', tastes that Liccy shared.[8] As in Lilian Hellman's apartment a lifetime earlier, Roald did not speak to her; before she left, he broke his silence and invited her to join him and Pat for dinner. Liccy declined. Again, as with his earlier pursuit of Pat, Roald waited then issued a second invitation. Like Pat, second time round Liccy agreed. Then work forced her to cancel. Instead, it was she who invited the Dahls to supper in her flat in Battersea. That night, Roald suggested meeting again when Pat was away. Liccy mentioned a forthcoming assignment in Paris; Roald set her a trap. He asked her to collect an umbrella from his former girlfriend Annabella, who was now living in France.

To Annabella, his accomplice, he explained his feelings. In the absence of any umbrella, Annabella reported what Roald had told her to a partly unsuspecting Liccy. When Roald and Liccy next met – for dinner at Roald's favourite gambling club, the Curzon House Club in Mayfair – Pat was away. The affair begun that night lasted ten years.

In a commercial for Anacin painkillers, shot in the year of her divorce, Pat tells viewers, 'The joys of this world belong to the fighters.' The first fight was not hers but Roald's and Liccy's – to keep their relationship a secret and sufficiently contained that it did not destroy Roald's marriage. Their success was short-lived. Roald's last-minute decision, in the summer of 1974, to holiday in Minorca rather than Norway was a means of seeing Liccy, whose rented house was close to the Dahls'. Liccy was accompanied by her daughters and a friend. Pat boasted of the happiness of her marriage and her sex life. At least one disbelieving glance, too tardily averted, provided the alert for which, subconsciously, she may have been looking.

It was the teenage Tessa, however, who had forced Roald to an openness of sorts. Tessa had overheard a late-night telephone conversation between Roald and Liccy during one of Pat's absences. Against his sister Else's advice, she confronted her father. Roald reacted with fury, threatening to expel her from the house, his anger not simply a reaction to discovery but its damage to the view of himself he cherished as a lynchpin of his family. Then he insisted she speak to Liccy, who, as strong-willed as him, offered her the option of complicity or an ending of the affair, with all that this entailed for Roald. Inevitably, Tessa chose complicity. Roald made clear to Liccy as well as Tessa that he did not wish to divorce Pat and break up the family whose survival had consumed so many of his energies; confusingly he rhapsodized to Liccy the extent of his love for her, describing their times together as 'easily the best times of my own particular life'.[9]

At this moment of turmoil, when he understood the threat posed by his affair to the gossipy, rambunctious, messy, unconventional life of Gipsy House, Roald began work on a second novel that, like *Fantastic Mr Fox*, published in 1970, celebrated his own role at the heart of a united family. In *Danny the Champion of the World*, Danny's love for his Roald-like father is straightforward and wholehearted, and his admiration embraces the man as well as the parent: 'It was impossible to be bored in my father's company. He was too sparky a man for that. Plots and plans and new ideas came flying off him like sparks from a grindstone.'[10] Roald struggled to decide on the novel's setting; there was a moment of revelation, and 'all I had to do was look around my own garden. And there it was …'[11] He returned to a story he had published in the *New Yorker* in 1959, 'The Champion of the World', placing himself at the centre as Danny's father, in a lilting evocation of idealized, romantic, rakish country life, and made good the metaphor by setting it in the garden of Gipsy House, in the brightly painted gypsy caravan where all Roald's children had played. Did Pat or Tessa read the novel and wryly smile? 'It was impossible to be with [my father] for long without being surprised and astounded by one thing or another,' Danny tells the reader.[12] From the outset, his new story was a manifesto for parenting Roald-style: its first draft endorsed parents 'who make exciting things happen around you, and who do exciting things with you, and who lead you into splendid adventures' – indispensable, inspirational, unorthodox, committed parents like Roald. Although the novel would remain one of his favourites, he did not acknowledge its element of self-serving, which perhaps he concealed from himself, or note that the strength of his belief in its message precluded any need for his usual elements of fantasy. While he was working on it, Knopf published a quartet of short stories that would be Roald's last collection for adults: *Switch Bitch*. Two had been written the previous decade, but their preoccupation with sex, the bleakness of their view of women and their focus on male aggression and self-delusion suited Roald's current malaise.

Pat was lunching with the hapless Tessa when she confirmed her suspicions of Roald's affair in the summer of 1975. Her furious response forced an uncomfortable scene at Gipsy House in which she, Roald and Liccy attempted to rationalize their dilemma. Roald denied any desire for a divorce; he disclaimed a sexual component to his relationship with Liccy, asking instead to be allowed Liccy's companionship. And then, at this moment of impasse, Liccy withdrew from his life. She wrote to Pat, regretting, but not apologizing for, the unhappiness to which she had contributed. For two years, Roald and Liccy separated. In Roald's case, Liccy continued to occupy the bulk of his thoughts; he was irritable, impatient. He took refuge in fond, whimsical games with Ophelia and Lucy, perched on a ladder outside their bedroom window, pretending to be the BFG, whom he had introduced in *Danny the Champion of the World*, blowing dreams into the room through a bamboo cane, or teaching ten-year-old Lucy to drive in a creaking Morris van in the orchard; every night he read aloud or told stories to his youngest daughters, a habit begun for Olivia. In quiet moments he read – he told schoolchildren in New Zealand that 'an adult reader of books has a terrific advantage over the non-reader. Sooner or later, all of you are going to suffer some kind of loneliness or illness, and the comfort you will get from being "a book reader" …

will be terrific.'[13] Out of sight in his writing hut, where only Roald ventured and the curtains were always drawn, he struggled to immerse himself in work, comforted, as he had told a radio interviewer in 1970, that 'everything else in your life disappears and you look at your bit of paper and get completely lost in what you're doing' in the last and most enduring of his private sanctuaries, which he likened to a nest and a womb.[14] As his sixtieth birthday approached, he was aware of feeling older. He told Alfred Knopf that for nine months after he had finished *Danny* he wrote nothing; instead he spent his time gardening. 'It gets harder and harder to generate the momentum that is necessary for making a new book or story,' he confessed.[15] If it was an admission of difficulties, it was not yet tantamount to giving up. Roald was collecting material for a collection of stories for older children. Not all the pieces in *The Wonderful Story of Henry Sugar and Six More* were new, but the title story – about a playboy-turned-philanthropist, who was 'six feet two inches tall, but he wasn't really as good-looking as he thought he was' – was life-affirming, while a painful story of bullying, 'The Swan', included what felt like a rallying cry to himself: 'Some people, when they have taken too much and have been driven beyond the point of endurance, simply crumble and give up. There are others, though they are not many, who will for some reason always be unconquerable.'[16]

A hip replacement operation in March 1977 was a reminder that Roald himself was not physically unconquerable; nor was his emotional resilience indefatigable.

During his slow, painful convalescence, he felt more than usually neglected by Pat. He telephoned Liccy. Clandestine again, their affair began for a second time. Despite its secrecy, deceits and routine caesuras, it restored some of Roald's equanimity, a distraction from the barrenness of his broken relationship with Pat. Its high spirits coloured the book on which he worked throughout 1978, *My Uncle Oswald*, a novel-length schoolboy's joke about sex initiated by a request from *Playboy* for a story for its twenty-fifth anniversary issue in January 1979. That Roald enjoyed reinhabiting the mindset of this lecherous cosmopolitan roué, a nostalgic self-projection, was clear from his byzantine correspondence with his editor Bob Gottlieb, in which Gottlieb corrected historical inaccuracies and requested excisions, including fictional details of Stravinsky's penis, which he worried would distress the composer's widow; on television Roald referred to 'very rich men, who for some reason are all incredibly lecherous'.[17] Roald peppered his text with extravagant exaggerations of the sort he enjoyed most: 'I myself became rather partial to Bulgarian ladies of aristocratic stamp. They had, amongst other things, the most unusual tongues.'[18] And perhaps, in the novel's lush confines, he protested at the limits of his furtive relationship with Liccy: 'Lukewarm is no good. Hot is not good either. White hot and passionate is the only thing to be.'[19]

Pat recognized Roald's withdrawal from her but could not bring herself to consider the implications of their marriage ending. Life at Gipsy House was tense, cold, at times acrid, but husband and wife had been together for three decades. Pat frequently travelled to the States for lecture tours: 'I stand there for fifty minutes with my notes and tell them the story of my life. There are always plenty of questions at the end, so I guess it's a good story,' she told journalists.[20] Roald welcomed her absences and puzzled at her appetite for these jamborees. In 1980, she bought a house on Martha's Vineyard, off the Massachusetts coast. Roald visited once, the following summer. He liked neither the Vineyard nor Pat's life there. The visit served a useful purpose in helping him to order in his mind what it was he did like. As he wrote to Pat on his early return, he liked his life at Gipsy House. 'I like to sit quietly in Gipsy House which I adore, writing my books and stories which I adore more and playing snooker a couple of times a week which I also adore, and popping up to London twice a week to play blackjack for which I have a passion.'[21] He added that he loved Pat. He did not refer to Liccy. Even so, the extent of her exclusion from her husband's inventory of homely pleasures left Pat no lifeline of hope. That Christmas, during frigid family celebrations, she discovered that Roald had resumed his affair with Liccy. It was the beginning of the end.

For Roald, despite Liccy's return, the times were out of joint. He was rich, successful and, from 1979, thanks to a long-running series of television adaptations of his short stories called *Tales of the Unexpected*, which he introduced himself, a household name. It was not enough. As recently as 1973, he had described his children as 'marvellous and gay and happy': he would discover persuasive evidence to the contrary.[22] Although he had not protested strongly at Tessa's decision, aged fifteen, to leave Downe House, her boarding school near Newbury, her subsequent rackety lifestyle irritated him, redeemed in part by the birth of her daughter, Sophie, in 1977. His speech at Tessa's wedding in February 1981 gave some indication of her unsettledness: 'Although she is still only in her early twenties, she has already had more jobs than the average person has in a lifetime – an actress, a model, an antique dealer, a landlady, a sort of pimp for plumbers and painters, and has run a Nannies Agency.'[23] Undoubtedly, Roald acknowledged the extent to which Tessa was a victim of family traumas. At Downe House he had written to her daily, 'day-to-day things – what the dogs were doing, funny things at home', transforming everyday domesticities into stories, his means of reassuring Tessa

of her fixity at the heart of the family.[24] Until he learned
of Lucy's cocaine addiction, when she was sixteen, he
imagined his younger children – born after Theo's accident
and Olivia's death, and too young to remember Pat's strokes
– had escaped the scourge of family tragedy. Roald blamed
himself for Lucy's addiction, but after her expulsion from
school for arson, sent her to London to live with Tessa,
who also struggled with addiction, a questionable decision
attributed by Lucy to his lack of empathy for teenagers.
Above all, Roald appeared blind to Theo's unhappiness. At
Tessa's wedding, Roald restated his conviction that 'action
is always better than words', a surprising apothegm for a
writer and a prescription unlikely to nurture marital bliss.[25]
In this same vigorous, unreflective spirit, he set up teenage
Theo as a baker and, when this failed, an antiques dealer;
Theo was happier working in the local supermarket. Roald's
initiatives for his son cost him £100,000 and caused gentle
Theo, always eager to please him, much anxiety. 'The secret
of my mother was minding her own business and always
being there if she's wanted,' Roald had told a radio journalist
during Sofie Magdalene's lifetime.[26] In his own approach was
a combination of intervention, financial over-compensation
and emotional absenteeism.[27] In Gipsy House, all plans
emanated from Roald, but his unilateral approach was not
always guided by insight or sensitivity. In a house of several

daughters, in which his sisters, nieces and nephews were daily visitors, and live-in cook-housekeepers, employed for a year at a time, became honorary family members, Roald exerted a paternal dominance. Or, as observers noted, lion-like he was the pride male among his seraglio of lionesses: attentive, protective, lordly.

Roald had increased his disaffection by inadvertently forfeiting autonomy in his working life. In the late 1970s, he extended earlier arrangements made with Knopf intended to limit his income tax liability. The device he chose took the form of a Swiss-registered company to which Knopf agreed to pay Roald's very considerable outstanding royalty payments: in the interests of legality, Knopf required a pretext for payment. This pretext took the form of goods supplied by the company, namely new books by Roald, each of which would be paid a proportion of the royalties already earned in the form of an advance. Knopf decided to make payments in four instalments; Roald's agreement committed him to supplying four new books, beginning with *My Uncle Oswald*. The sooner he wanted the payments owed him, the faster he would be required to provide each new manuscript. It was not how Roald was accustomed to work, and he quickly discovered that it was not his preferred way of working.

With an increasingly bad grace, he produced two short children's novels and a book of children's verse, *Dirty Beasts*.

In *The Twits*, delivered late in 1979, and *George's Marvellous Medicine*, which he completed the following spring, Roald's testiness shaped tales of gruesome mischief. 'When writing stories, I cannot seem to rid myself of the unfortunate habit of having one person do nasty things to another person,' he told television viewers in his introduction to an episode of *Tales of the Unexpected* based on 'Neck'; in *The Twits*, husband and wife compete with one another in fervid nastiness. *George's Marvellous Medicine* returns to the theme of *The Night Digger*, an innocent carer (the eight-year-old George of the title) in thrall to an exacting invalid, 'that grizzly old grunion of a Grandma'.[28] George, however, turns the tables on his curmudgeonly gaoler; Roald's narrative is devoid of pity for Grandma's sorry fate. The novel culminates in simple if satisfying didacticism. 'That's what happens to you if you're grumpy and bad-tempered,' George's father tells him, as father and son watch Grandma's demise by shrinking.[29] It was not a lesson Roald himself took to heart. Over the two years of the contract's lifespan, his attitude towards all and everyone involved in publishing the books he decided he had been tricked into writing soured into verbal fist-shaking and foot-stamping acrimony. At the time of Tessa's wedding, he announced he was considering leaving Knopf. The threat was by way of a trump card, typical of Roald's behaviour at its intimidating worst, and he did not intend to be taken at his word. Goaded, bullied and exasperated, Knopf exacted revenge as formidable as George's: 'You have behaved to us in a way I can honestly say is unmatched in my experience for overbearingness and utter lack of civility,' wrote Roald's former editor Bob Gottlieb on 5 March: 'Let me reverse your threat: unless you start acting civilly to us, there is no possibility of our agreeing to publish you.'[30] Three decades earlier, Alfred Knopf had pursued and wooed the author of a story called 'Taste'. But Knopf himself had retired from the company he sold to Random House in 1960; he could not shield Roald from the effects of his bad behaviour. A partnership between author and publishing house, sealed the year that Roald married Pat with publication of *Someone Like You*, unravelled in tandem with their marriage. The spirit of his departure moved Roald to fury rather than sadness: he did not quickly forget Random House's perfidy.

Nor did he allow abrasive severance to interfere with his work, a measure in itself of the toughness at the core of Roald's character, as well as his capacity for self-immolation in what he called his 'dotty world of fantasy': 'Nothing can prevent the old fires of excitement rekindling once I am well into a story,' he wrote, not even treacherous Random House.[31] He spent much of 1981 writing a story of two innocents battling giant-size bullies that would become his favourite of his children's books. The BFG had made an appearance in *Danny the Champion of the World*, as well as the bedtime rituals of Ophelia and Lucy. Over the course of the year, the gentle, dream-catching giant occupied his author, Roald calculated, for 600 hours. The story's roots are of longer emergence. *The BFG* came closer than any of Roald's previous children's books to the folklore of his childhood: it describes the defeat of a race of cruel, flesh-eating giants by an orphan child, who is helped by a friendly giant and a queen. Seamlessly, the story moves between real and imaginary worlds; the BFG's distinctively mangled speech merges the everyday and the fantastical. Magic pervades the novel, as it would all of Roald's later full-length children's stories, the BFG himself its mouthpiece, urging both Sophie and the novel's readers to believe. 'Just because we happen not to have actually *seen* something with our own two little winkles, we think it is not existing,' he upbraids a sceptical Sophie.[32] Like Roald, the BFG does not expect to be challenged, and more than once his advice to Sophie is simply to accept what she cannot understand: 'Dreams is full of mystery and magic,' the BFG said. 'Do not try to understand them.'[33]

During the period of Pat's recovery, Roald had made notes of her neologisms. Twenty years later, he did not acknowledge her inspiration behind the most distinctive voice in his fiction. The year of the book's publication, Pat agreed to a divorce and returned to the States. Legalities were finalized the following summer. An interviewer questioned Roald. His reply was characteristic, suggesting action as a remedy for unhappiness – and then apportioning blame: 'It's very sad and knocks you out after thirty years … I don't think one ever gets over anything, death of a child, divorce. You have just got to go on and every year that goes by helps. The longer you live the more you become aware that the world is full of stinkers.'[34] On 15 December 1983, at the age of sixty-seven, Roald married Liccy.

X

WE SO LOVED
BEING WITH YOU
1983–1990

'Even in my old age I'm always winning.'

'I USED TO TRAVEL around quite a bit, talking to teachers and schools,' Roald wrote on 28 January 1985, in response to a child's invitation to visit her school in Bromsgrove, 'but I'm now 68 years old with two steel hips and a spine that is beginning to act up on me after six laminectomies, therefore bucketing around the country does me no good at all.'[1] Increasingly Roald would complain about his physical creakiness, but the seven years of his marriage to Liccy were to prove remarkably fertile, producing, among other writings, a series of bestselling novels for children and successful forays into fictionalized autobiography.

In 1983, the novel Roald had dedicated to Liccy won the Whitbread Children's Book Award; *The Witches* also prompted accusations of misogyny. Roald was unperturbed. None of its characters loomed larger for him than the grandmother: based on an elderly Sofie Magdalene, a hieratic figure in her wheelchair in the conservatory of her annexe at Else's house, her long hair coiled on top of her head, he imagined her 'tremendously old and wrinkled, with a massive wide body which was smothered in grey lace ... majestic in her armchair, filling every inch of it'.[2] His most frightening story in its graphic portrayal of the witches' malevolence and their ugliness, *The Witches* was also, as Roald knew, his most tender. The love between the boy and his grandmother, which survives the boy's transformation into a mouse, moved Roald as much as any of his readers. Outside the novel, even marriage to Liccy did not immediately bring Roald that respite the mouse-boy enjoys, where he 'shut [his] eyes and thought of nothing and felt at peace with the world'.[3] Instead, after turbulent decades, it yielded orderliness – emotional as well as physical – in which his genius flourished: his last years witnessed creative and commercial apotheosis, including children's fiction of lasting merit. In the summer of 1988, Roald wrote a poem, 'Where art thou, Mother Christmas?', for a Christmas card to raise funds for Great Ormond Street Hospital: such was his popularity that printers Richard Clay Limited agreed to print a million of the cards for free. In January 1990, *Matilda*, *Danny the Champion of the World*, *The BFG* and *The Witches* occupied the first four places in *The Bookseller*'s chart of bestselling children's fiction; figures sent to Roald at the beginning of that month calculated his paperback sales for the previous year at 2,383,518 books. Success on this scale transformed him into a publishing phenomenon. His marriage to Liccy transformed him in other ways: he became less testy, more demonstrative, as serene as an immoderate nature that revelled in provocation could be.

Forcefully he continued to dominate his family. In public, he theorized extensively on the craft of writing for children, magus-like in his pronouncements. He craved public honours, in particular a knighthood, and literary esteem. Denied both – in 1985 he turned down the lesser award of an OBE – he insisted that writing for children outstripped the difficulties of adult fiction and that, in his own case, he enjoyed special insight into children's thoughts and feelings. His riposte to the critics who ignored him was lofty dismissal: 'I make things to please children. I don't care about grown-ups,' he wrote, not quite truthfully.[4] Happiness did not entirely temper his irascibility or heedless bullish combativeness. He remained egotistical. In 1988, he instructed the National Curriculum English Working Group that 'all teachers should read passages of good literature to their classes, right up to age sixteen. Choose an absorbing, well-written short story that is guaranteed to hold the attention of the class.' Among the five examples he recommended was a story of his own from *Someone Like You*.[5] He was vainglorious: even his dreams were of victories, as he told an interviewer in 1988:

I spend my life having dreams of glory. Even in my old age I'm always winning the golf open championships or tennis at Wimbledon or something like that. I go through long thinks about this, lying in the dark when I'm … trying to get to sleep in bed. Every little detail of what happens … [I] dream up that I've beaten them all and everyone's surprised.[6]

He continued to court controversy, including to his own detriment, most notably in the polemic he published in the *Literary Review* in August 1983. A review of an illustrated account of the recent invasion of Beirut by Israel, it was a heartfelt but misconceived protest. In the short term, it earned Roald obloquy from several quarters, even death threats; in the long term, the shadow of anti-Semitism would generate opprobrium that continues today and, late in 2020, forced an apology from Roald's family on his official website. Neither short- nor long-term reaction had been Roald's intention: he was clear, he claimed, that his dislike was for Israel not Jews. In a letter to *The Times*, he explained, 'I am anti-Israeli now because I am anti-killing, and in recent years they have killed more human beings than any other country on earth.' He added that he himself had 'quite a few pints of Jewish blood in my own veins through my Norwegian grandmother, Hesselberg, and my great-great-grandfather, who was called Preuss'.[7] Not everyone accepted a distinction that suggests equivocation. Statements throughout his life do indeed suggest antipathy to Jews: as long ago as 1951, Ann Watkins had suggested Roald modify the anti-Jewishness of characters in

Fifty Thousand Frogskins.[8] As the controversy gathered momentum in the late summer of 1983, Roald fanned the flames: to the *New Statesman* he described 'a trait in the Jewish character that does provoke a certain animosity, maybe it's a kind of lack of generosity towards non-Jews … Even a stinker like Hitler didn't just pick on them for no reason.'[9] Six years later, he adopted a similarly obstreperous, uncompromising stance after again jumping into hot water. In another letter to *The Times*, criticizing Salman Rushdie when *The Satanic Verses* earned the novelist a fatwa, Roald compared Rushdie unfavourably to Degas, 'who had more art in his little fingernail than Rushdie has in his entire body'.[10] To observers, Roald appeared to cultivate conflict and abrasiveness: outside sensitive areas, its effect was not always to give offence. Ahead of a visit to Gipsy House by journalist Angela Levin, Roald set out the terms of their meeting: 'We'll chat, I'll give you a grotty omelette and it would help if you bugger off soon after two.'[11] Levin recognized the posturing behind his curmudgeonliness.

Despite divisiveness, Roald's last years were more often characterized by partnerships. In place of the vanished relationships with his mother, Charles Marsh, who had died in 1964, and Pat, Roald remained close to his sisters, all of whom lived within easy reach of Gipsy House. His marriage to Liccy sustained him on many levels: 'She fed him with such affection and cared for him with so much devotion that his heart sang,' Tessa wrote fulsomely; 'it is she we must give thanks to for *Matilda*'.[12] A neighbour suggested that Liccy's gift to Roald was 'inner peace': it did not preclude what Liccy herself cautiously labelled rattiness.[13] For others, Roald glowed with his love for her. Liccy's redecoration of Gipsy House, extending to significant remodelling (much to Roald's chagrin at the time), ultimately imposed the well-ordered tranquillity a tired, older Roald needed and craved.[14] The unabashed admiration, support and guidance of Roald's long-term editor at Jonathan Cape, Tom Maschler, and, for a briefer period, the obsessive, enthusiastic, constructive 'super-editing' of Stephen Roxburgh at his American publishers Farrar, Straus & Giroux, facilitated and fine-tuned the burst of creative energy that may have surprised Roald himself and accounted for new titles in his run of what were by now spectacularly successful children's books – among them *Matilda* quickly attained the classic status of *Charlie and the Chocolate Factory*, *Danny the Champion of the World* and *The BFG*. Roald's working partnership with illustrator Quentin Blake, initiated by Maschler in the late 1970s, when Blake was still at the Royal College of Art and Maschler commissioned illustrations for *The Enormous Crocodile*, enriched his children's books, expressing in a different idiom their combination of otherworldly mischief and spirited fantasy, and came to invest a disparate output with visual coherence.

Neither the admiration of his collaborators nor Liccy's loving kindness, however, could lessen Roald's physical suffering. Pain had become a way of life. In 1981, he told Pat he was 'never out of it unless I am sitting or lying down, and then only half the time'; inevitably its impact was more than physical.[15] That he was frequently bedridden may have prompted the backward glance that colours much of his later writing. Stephen Roxburgh had only recently completed detailed and comprehensive work on Roald's manuscript of *The BFG* when Roald had presented him with the second full-length children's novel Roxburgh edited, *The Witches*. As first written, the novel had begun with a fictionalized retelling of Roald's childhood. Some details remain in the published novel, like the boy's pleasure in his treehouse that recalls the secret thrills Roald experienced as an eight-year-old diary writer hiding aloft from his sisters: 'It was lovely being high up there in that conker tree, all alone with the pale young leaves coming out everywhere around me'; the flavour of Roald's childhood emerges in pre-war slang: 'That's perfectly beastly!'[16] Roxburgh's decision to separate much of the autobiographical material from Roald's fictional plot, itself partly inspired by Sofie Magdalene's long ago tales of witches and hags, had enabled him to suggest to

Roald an alternative use for these sections of his manuscript, namely two volumes of autobiography written for his child readers. Over the next three years these became *Boy* and *Going Solo*, swashbuckling narratives of Roald's life up to 1942, published in 1984 and 1986 respectively. In both, Roald exaggerated real-life events in line with his habit of 'mak[ing] the Truth a little more interesting': the books took no account of grey areas.[17] Roald justified his approach by insisting that children 'tend to see things in black and white', much as he did himself.[18]

Time and again, this was true of his outlook on the world around him. His polarized perspective – clear in his statements about Israel – generated conflict in Roald's friendships, among his family and in relationships in his working life. Like his association with his last Knopf editor, Bob Gottlieb, Roald's partnership with Stephen Roxburgh unravelled. Roxburgh's response to Roald's last full-length children's novel, *Matilda*, sounded the death knell. In its first draft, the story bore few resemblances to the novel that was eventually published: there was a rough, sketchy, unfinished quality to the writing and construction, and the story, about a wicked little girl rigging a horse race, lacked charm. Roald knew this, but did not consider it Roxburgh's place to make clear the extent to which he shared this view. Three times Roxburgh travelled from New York to Buckinghamshire to work on the novel with Roald; the process exhausted Roald, and the two men argued. In the finished manuscript, Matilda recognizes, 'as Napoleon once said', that 'the only sensible thing to do when you are attacked is … to counter-attack'.[19] With his revisions complete, Roald counter-attacked, quibbling over contractual details. It provided him with a reason to leave Farrar, Straus & Giroux and escape Roxburgh's cool appraisal, which had hurt (and irritated) him. Instead Viking published *Matilda* in America. Its remarkable popularity on both sides of the Atlantic vindicated both men: as rewritten, the novel benefited from Roxburgh's editorial eye as well as Roald's fund of invention and feeling. *Matilda*, Roald told the Secretary of State for Education, Kenneth Baker, sold 'well over 100,000 copies' in hardback in its first year; paperback sales exceeded 500,000 in six months.[20]

The benignity of Roald's second marriage enabled him to enjoy the pleasures he had described to Pat in the letter he wrote on his return from Martha's Vineyard. He spent most of his time at Gipsy House, its walls hung with the mirrors he had restored twenty years ago and a collection of paintings that thrilled him, 'complimentary newspaper reviews, poems by his children ... spectacular collages by children all over the world based on many of his books' and the enormous calendar that hung behind the dining room door; when he was well enough, seven days a week he walked the narrow garden path to his writing hut, with its bright yellow door, carrying with him a flask of coffee.[21] Public prominence and commercial success kept Roald's post bag full. At the long pine table in the dining room, his Jack Russell, Chopper, sitting on his knee, he dictated responses to his secretary, Wendy Kress; he continued to reply to many of the letters sent to him by children and teachers, evolving a formula to amuse: 'Hello, handsome Mr Johnson, and all the clever children who wrote me such lovely letters.'[22] His letters, like his books, sought to enter fully into a child's world, devoid of cynicism, full of magic: he told the seven-year-old girl who, inspired by *The BFG*, sent him one of her dreams in a bottle in February 1989, 'You are the first person in the world who has sent me one of these and it intrigued me very much. I also liked the dream. Tonight I shall go down to the village and blow it through the bedroom window of some sleeping child and see if it works.'[23] Author Brough Girling invited Roald to become chairman of a school-based reading campaign, Readathon: Roald agreed 'as long as I don't have to do anything'.[24] Letters arrived from the parents of children in hospital: in return

Roald dispatched copies of his books, signed books sent to him, or suggested a visit when the child was well enough. 'If it would help to cheer her up, you could by all means pop over here and I will sign her books,' he wrote to a mother whose daughter was suffering from chronic renal failure.[25] Olivia's death never left him. In 1988, he wrote a letter for a pamphlet produced by public health authorities in England, encouraging parents to have their children vaccinated against measles. He described the rapid course of Olivia's death and his attachment to her memory:

> I dedicated two of my books to Olivia, the first was *James and the Giant Peach*. That was when she was still alive. The second was *The BFG*, dedicated to her memory after she had died from measles. You will see her name at the beginning of each of these books. And I know how happy she would be if only she could know that her death had helped to save a good deal of illness and death among other children.

There was to be one last tragedy: the death, as a result of an aneurysm caused by an undiagnosed brain tumour, of Liccy's youngest daughter, Lorina, in February 1990. She was twenty-seven. Liccy's devastation, like his own at Olivia's death, could not be remedied by Roald's doctrine of 'doing'.

In hindsight, his family came to regard Lorina's death as signposting Roald's own descent: in its aftermath the pace of his physical decline appeared to quicken. His bones ached, he was troubled by problems with his eyes. Liccy remained his lodestar, both the centre and the substance of his world. His decision, announced bluntly to his children – with predictable repercussions – that he would leave everything to Liccy was evidence of his devotion to her, as well as the trust he placed in her. He knew that, after his death, life would not imitate art: Liccy was not the stepmother of fairytales or Roald-style stories, she would share her inheritance with his four children, as indeed she has. He asked his daughter Ophelia to write his official biography, a task she accepted but did not complete.

Roald finished his last children's book, *The Minpins*, a romantic, lyrical, otherworldly story, over the course of 1990; he described it as 'a sort of fairy-tale'. Suffering from anaemia, 'a bit off colour … feeling sleepy when I shouldn't have been and without that lovely old bubbly energy that drives one to write books and drink gin and chase after girls', he marshalled all his faltering energies to complete it.[26] Tests revealed that Roald was suffering from a form of leukaemia called myelofibrosis, for which there was no certain cure. His response was steadfast. Once he had held in check any pity he felt for Pat in her illness; he did not succumb to self-pity now. Indeed he may have underestimated the odds he battled. His introduction to the Roald Dahl Newsletter, written in August 1990, had an upbeat quality:

I'm told that if my bone-marrow factory refuses to go back to work properly they can still go on topping me up like this more or less for ever, anyway for quite a few more years. So don't put me into the grave quite yet. I usually manage to climb out again. I've done it many times before.[27]

In the event the illness moved quickly: by the autumn his hospital stays were repeated and frequent. He was admitted to the John Radcliffe Hospital in Oxford for the last time in the middle of November and died in the early hours of the morning on 22 November. His final full-length sentence offered shreds of comfort to those around the bedside: 'I'm not frightened. It's just that I will miss you all so much.'[28] Like the Giraffe and the Pelly and Me in the story of the same name that he wrote for younger readers in 1984, he might have added, 'We so loved being with you.'

His affairs were in order, including, over the course of this final year, a reconciliation with Pat of her instigating, and at the end he kept faith with the uncomplaining philosophy to which he had clung throughout a life whose rich rewards had been balanced by searing vicissitudes: 'Life, after all, is exactly like a game of snakes-and-ladders, full of pitfalls as well as surprises, and we simply have to learn to cope with them both.'[29]

Only the man had died – husband, father, brother: his work lived on. Despite her devastation, Liccy had no choice but to apply herself to Roald's public legacy and administration of his literary estate. She admitted her shock at his death in a letter written soon afterwards, adding that 'life must go on and I am starting a Roald Dahl Foundation, which we hope to get off the ground in a year-and-a-half's time.'[30] In the thirty years since its inception, the Foundation, later renamed Roald Dahl's Marvellous Children's Charity and, since 2017, under royal patronage, has funded eighty specialist nurses supporting and caring for seriously ill children across the United Kingdom.

Months before his death, Tessa described her father as 'an immensely important writer who, for the last 20 years, has filled children with spark and imagination.'[31] Others – mostly outside the literary establishment, which rejected Roald's claim that writing for children outstripped the demands of adult fiction – readily agreed, and have continued to do so. The Roald Dahl Children's Gallery in Aylesbury, which opened in his adopted Buckinghamshire in 1996, the plaza named after him in 2000 in Cardiff, the city of his birth, and a series of commemorative stamps issued by the Royal Mail in 2012 testify to Roald's posthumous renown and continuing popularity. In 2016, the centenary of his birth was widely celebrated. Among Christmas television offerings that year was the BBC's animated version of *Revolting Rhymes*, while 'The Great Mouse Plot', part of *Boy*, published as a stand-alone World Book Day title, comfortably outsold its competitors. By 2016, it was no longer possible to detail Roald's sales figures with any accuracy: *The Bookseller* suggested 'a conservative estimate' of more than 250 million books, with the author's titles in print in fifty-eight languages across the globe.[32] Two years earlier, however, the Royal Mint Advisory Committee had rejected plans for a centenary coin issue on the grounds that Roald was 'associated with antisemitism and not regarded as an author of the highest reputation.'[33]

Sensibilities in the third decade of the twenty-first century differ markedly from those of the pre-war world of Roald's childhood, when he listened on Sofie Magdalene's knee to nursery rhymes and Norse folklore, stories by Beatrix Potter and Hilaire Belloc's *Cautionary Tales*, and through teachers including Mrs O'Connor and John Crommelin-Brown first encountered classic works in a literary canon that has since been challenged and in part reordered. In this altered climate, liberal shibboleths have little truck with former renown; his detractors question the continuance of Roald's prominence. The stain of anti-Semitism will not disappear; there will be other accusations, also damaging. But in September 2021, streaming giant Netflix acquired from Roald's family the Roald Dahl Story Company, including the rights to *Charlie and the Chocolate Factory*, *Danny the Champion of the World*, *The BFG* and *Matilda*, for a sum reportedly 'a little over' £500 million.[34] 'Good novels are essential to most of us,' wrote the schoolboy Roald in an essay about children's reading.[35] They became his life's work and remain his lasting legacy.

Endnotes

Introduction: 'A Perfectly Ordinary Fellow'

1 Roald Dahl, 'For Children', speech, typescript 1975, the Roald Dahl Museum and Story Centre (hereafter RDMSC) RD06010126.
2 Liz Attenborough to Roald Dahl, 24 May 1990, RDMSC RD1/6/12.
3 P. L. Travers, 'Johnny Delaney', 1944, included in *Aunt Sass Christmas Stories* (Virago, London, 2014), p. 111.
4 Donald Sturrock, *Storyteller: The Life of Roald Dahl* (Harper Press paperback, London, 2011), p. 486.
5 Kathryn Hughes, *Guardian*, 11 September 2010.
6 Roald Dahl to Christine Wootton, 2 August 1989, private collection.
7 Roald Dahl to Professor Mark West, 6 April 1988, RDMSC RD1/6/10.
8 Dahl, 'For Children'.
9 Roald Dahl, 'A Note on writing books for Children', RDMSC RD 6/2/1/12.

Chapter 1: 'Little Boy Blue'

1 Roald Dahl, 'On Writing *Matilda*', RDMSC RD/6/1/2/30.

2 Roald Dahl, 'Genesis and Catastrophe', 1959, reprinted in *The Complete Short Stories Volume Two* (Penguin, London, 2013), p. 105.

3 Roald Dahl, *Boy: Tales of Childhood* (Puffin paperback, London, 1986), p. 20.

4 Roald Dahl, *My Year* (New Windmill reprint, Oxford, 1997), p. 5.

5 *Western Mail*, 6 November 1918 and 22 November 1919.

6 Dahl, *Boy*, p. 53; Felicity and Roald Dahl, *Memories with Food at Gipsy House* (Viking, London, 1991), p. 65.

7 Roald Dahl, *Fantastic Mr Fox* (Puffin reprint, London, 1997), p. 17.

8 Dahl, *Boy*, p. 17; *Western Mail*, 30 October 1975.

9 Dahl, *Boy*, p. 21.

10 Tessa Dahl, 'You Can Love but You'd Better Not Touch', *YOU Magazine*, 1990, RDMSC RD/12/2/11/1.

11 Roald Dahl, 'A Dose of Dahl's Magic Medicine', audio interview, 28 September 1986, RDMSC RD/12/1/27; Roald Dahl to the secretary, Writers Guild of America, 9 January 1984, RDMSC RD1/6/6.

12 Tessa Dahl, 'You Can Love but You'd Better Not Touch'; Wendy Kress, quoted Sturrock, *Storyteller*, p. 553.

13 Dahl, *Boy*, p. 22.

14 Dahl, *My Year*, pp. 18 and 20.

15 Roald Dahl, 'The Bookseller', 1987, reprinted in *The Complete Short Stories Volume Two*, p. 752.

16 Roald Dahl, *The Witches* (Puffin reprint, London, 1985), p. 8.

17 Else Logsdail (sister), quoted in 'A Dose of Dahl's Magic Medicine'.

18 Jeremy Treglown, *Roald Dahl: A Biography* (Faber and Faber, London, 1994), p. 14.

19 Roald Dahl, 'Only This', 1944, reprinted in *The Complete Short Stories Volume One* (Penguin, London, 2013), p. 38.

20 Alfhild Hansen (sister), quoted in Sturrock, Donald, *Love from Boy: Roald Dahl's Letters to His Mother* (John Murray, London, 2016), p. xxi.

21 Alfhild Hansen (sister), quoted in 'A Dose of Dahl's Magic Medicine'.

22 Roald Dahl, Ideas Book 1, RDMSC RD11/1.

23 Else Logsdail (sister), quoted in 'A Dose of Dahl's Magic Medicine'; Dahl, *The Witches*, p. 6; see Roald Dahl, Introduction, *Fear* (Penguin reprint, London, 2017), p. 12.

24 Roald Dahl, 'Nursery Rhymes', school essay, *c.*1930s, RDMSC RD13/3/39.

25 Roald Dahl, *Charlie and the Chocolate Factory* (Puffin reprint, London, 2001), p. 97.

26 Dahl, Ideas Book 1.

27 Roald Dahl, 'Joss Spivvis', included in *When We Were Young: Memories of Childhood* (David & Charles, Newton Abbot, 1987), p. 13.

28 Damian Walford Davies, ed., *Roald Dahl: Wales of the Unexpected* (University of Wales Press, Cardiff, 2016), p. 17.

29 Ibid., p. 16; Dahl, 'Joss Spivvis', p. 14.

30 Dahl, 'Joss Spivvis', p. 13.

31 Sturrock, *Storyteller*, p. 68.

32 Roald Dahl, 'Dahl Diary', manuscript, RDMSC RD2/33/4.

33 Dahl, *Boy*, p. 54.

34 Ibid., pp. 55–6.

35 Ibid., p. 57.

36 Ibid., p. 61.

37 Roald Dahl, *James and the Giant Peach* (Puffin reprint, London, 2016), p. 1.

38 Roald Dahl, *Danny the Champion of the World* (Puffin reprint, London, 2001), p. 215.
39 Roald Dahl, 'Dreams', school essay, *c.*1930s, RDMSC RD13/3/3/23.
40 Dahl, *Boy*, p. 65.
41 Roald Dahl, *The BFG* (Puffin reprint, London, 2016), p. 14.
42 Sturrock, *Love from Boy*, p. 22.
43 Ibid., p. 4; Roald Dahl, *Matilda* (Puffin reprint, London, 2013), p. 77.
44 Roald Dahl, 'On Writing *Matilda*', RDMSC RD/6/1/2/30.
45 Ibid.; Sturrock, *Storyteller*, p. 55.
46 Sturrock, *Love from Boy*, p. 29.
47 Dahl, *Boy*, p. 51; Roald Dahl, 'Lucky Break', 1977, reprinted in *The Complete Short Stories Volume Two*, p. 618.
48 Dahl, 'Lucky Break', p. 618.
49 Dahl, *Boy*, p. 49.
50 Ibid., p. 33.
51 Dahl, 'Dahl Diary'.
52 Ibid.
53 Ibid.
54 Ibid.
55 Ibid.
56 Ibid.
57 Dahl, 'Lucky Break', p. 624.
58 Ibid., p. 619; Dahl, *The Witches*, p. 71.
59 Dahl, 'Lucky Break', p. 621.
60 Dahl, 'Dahl Diary'.
61 Sturrock, *Storyteller*, p. 56.
62 Roald Dahl, letter to the editor of *The Times*, 9 October 1989, RDMSC RD1/6/19.
63 Roald Dahl, 'A Note on Writing Books for Children', RDMSC RD6/2/1/12.

64 Dahl, *Matilda*, p. 7.
65 Sturrock, *Storyteller*, p. 56; Roald Dahl, Introduction, *Fear*, p. 11.
66 Sturrock, *Love from Boy*, p. 199.
67 Dahl, 'A Note on Writing Books for Children'.
68 Roald Dahl to Kenneth Baker, 21 November 1988, RDMSC RD010613.
69 Dahl, 'Lucky Break', p. 629.
70 Roald Dahl, Foreword to 'The Roald Dahl Notebook', RDMSC RD1/6/11.

Chapter 2: Plodding, Endless Terms

1 See RDMSC RD13/4/8.
2 Roald Dahl to Sofie Magdalene Dahl, 4 February 1934, RDMSC RD13/1/9/24.
3 Sturrock, *Love from Boy*, p. 32.
4 Roald Dahl to Sofie Magdalene Dahl, 25 January 1930. See Sturrock, *Love from Boy*, p. 45.
5 Ibid., p. 85.
6 Ibid., p. 56.
7 See RDMSC RD2/23/1/166.
8 Ibid.; Dahl, *Boy*, p. 163.
9 Dahl, *My Year*, p. 44.
10 Roald Dahl, 'The Reapers', c.1930s, RDMSC RD13/3/3/13.
11 Roald Dahl, 'Laughter', school essay, October 1933, RDMSC RD13/3/3/1.
12 Dahl, 'Lucky Break', p. 630.
13 See RDMSC RD2/23/1/166.
14 Dahl, *Danny the Champion of the World*, p. 6.
15 Roald Dahl, 'Galloping Foxley', 1953, reprinted in *The Complete Short Stories Volume One*, p. 445.

16 Treglown, *Roald Dahl*, p. 22.

17 Dahl, *Boy*, p. 145.

18 Roald Dahl to 'all the clever children at Primate Dixon Memorial Boys' School', undated [1988], later included as 'A Poem in Reply to Schoolchildren', in *The Roald Dahl Treasury* (Jonathan Cape, London, 1997).

19 Sturrock, *Storyteller*, p. 79.

20 Ibid., p. 53.

21 Roald Dahl, annotation to a school essay on 'The Importance of Parliamentary Reform Acts', c.1930s, RDMSC RD13/3/3/4.

22 Roald Dahl to Sofie Magdalene Dahl, May 1933, RDMSC RD 13/1/8/38.

23 Roald Dahl, 'Adventures with Carlyle's Wishing Hat', school essay, c.1930s, RDMSC RD13/3/3/10.

24 Roald Dahl, 'A Conversation with a Pavement Artist', creative writing, c.1930s, RDMSC RD13/3/3/6.

25 See RDMSC RD/12/1/27.

26 Dahl, *Boy*, p. 163.

27 Ibid., p. 148.

28 Roald Dahl, see Angela Levin, *YOU Magazine*, 24 April 1983, RDMSC RD12/1/16.

29 Roald Dahl, 'Decisive Episodes of British Rule in India up to 1857', school essay, c.1930s, RDMSC RD13/3/3/17.

30 Roald Dahl to Sofie Magdalene Dahl, undated, RDMSC RD13/1/6/48.

31 Dahl, 'Lucky Break', p. 621.

32 Ibid.

33 John Crommelin-Brown, *Dies Heroica* (Hodder & Stoughton, London, 1918), p. v.

34 Ibid., p. 21.

35 See annotation to Roald Dahl, creative writing, 'Getting the News', c.1930s, RDMSC RD13/3/3/16.
36 See annotation to Roald Dahl, 'Laughter', school essay, c.1930s, RDMSC RD13/3/3/1.
37 See RDMSC RD6/2/1/23.
38 Roald Dahl to Jay Williams, undated (1980); Roald Dahl to Professor Brian Cox, Department of Education and Science, 2 June 1988, RDMSC RD2/6/88.
39 Dahl, 'For Children'.
40 Roald Dahl, 'An African Story', 1945, reprinted in *The Complete Short Stories Volume One*, p. 63.
41 See RDMSC RD/12/1/27.
42 Roald Dahl, 'Mr Billy Bubbler', see RDMSC RD11/3/23/1-11.
43 Roald Dahl, 'A Conversation with a Pavement Artist', creative writing, c.1930s, RDMSC RD13/3/3/6; Dahl, *Boy*, p. 166.
44 Sturrock, *Storyteller*, p. 581, note 42.
45 Dahl, *My Year*, p. 44.
46 RDMSC RD13/12/90.
47 Dahl, 'For Children'.
48 Ibid.

Chapter 3: Fit and Tough

1 Roald Dahl, 'Newfoundland Diary', RDMSC RD13/5/1.
2 George Murray Levick, *Journal of the Royal Society of Arts*, 4 August 1939, p. 970.
3 Sturrock, *Love from Boy*, p. 85.
4 Ibid., p. 90.
5 Ibid., p. 88.
6 Ibid., p. 67.

7 Roald Dahl, 'Newfoundland Diary', 19 August 1934, RDMSC RD13/5/1.

8 Ibid., 18 August 1934.

9 Ibid., 26 August 1934.

10 Ibid., 20 August 1934.

11 Ibid., 26 August 1934.

12 Roald Dahl, in 'A Dose of Dahl's Magic Medicine'.

13 Dahl, *Boy*, p. 170.

14 See Lucy Hughes-Hallett, 'Roald Dahl: Tall Storyteller', *Vogue*, 1979.

15 Treglown, *Roald Dahl*, p. 30.

16 Roald Dahl, *Going Solo* (Puffin reprint, London, 1988), pp. 3, 23.

17 See Jeremy Treglown, 'The Fantastic Mr Dahl', *Smithsonian Magazine*, July 2016.

18 *Western Mail*, 10–15 December 1937.

19 Dahl, *Going Solo*, p. 5.

20 Ibid., p. 26.

21 Sturrock, *Love from Boy*, p. 106.

22 Ibid.

23 Roald Dahl to Sofie Magdalene Dahl, undated [January 1939], RDMSC RD14/3/19; Sturrock, *Love from Boy*, p. 115.

24 Ibid.

25 Ibid.

26 Dahl, *Boy*, p. 247.

27 Dahl, *Going Solo*, p. 26.

28 Sturrock, *Love from Boy*, p. 105.

29 Dahl, *Going Solo*, p. 23.

30 Roald Dahl, *The Minpins* (Puffin reprint, London, 2017), p. 98.

31 Sturrock, *Love from Boy*, p. 120.

32 Roald Dahl, 'Claud's Dog', 1953, reprinted in *The Complete Short Stories Volume One*, p. 519.

33 Sturrock, *Love from Boy*, p. 136.

34 Dahl, 'An African Story', p. 61.

35 Sturrock, *Storyteller*, p. 154.

36 Roald Dahl to Sofie Magdalene Dahl, 14 August 1940, RDMSC RD14/4/3; Roald Dahl, 'Madame Rosette', 1945, reprinted in *The Complete Short Stories Volume One*, p. 129.

37 Roald Dahl, 'The Surgeon', 1988, reprinted in *The Complete Short Stories Volume Two*, p. 782.

38 Dahl, *The Minpins*, pp. 67, 83; Roald Dahl, 'They Shall Not Grow Old', 1945, reprinted in *The Complete Short Stories Volume One*, p. 117.

39 Roald Dahl, 'Beware of the Dog', 1944, reprinted in *The Complete Short Stories Volume One*, p. 46.

40 Roald Dahl, 'A Piece of Cake', 1945, reprinted in *The Complete Short Stories Volume One*, p. 89.

41 Dahl, *James and the Giant Peach*, p. 101.

42 Dahl, 'A Piece of Cake', p. 92.

43 Dahl, *Boy*, p. 35.

Chapter 4: Stalky

1 Roald Dahl, 'Cinderella', *Revolting Rhymes* (Jonathan Cape, London, 1982).

2 See Roald Dahl to Sofie Magdalene Dahl, 17 April 1943, RDMSC RD14/5/2/11.

3 Felicity and Roald Dahl, *Memories with Food at Gipsy House*, p. 66.

4 Tom Solomon, *Roald Dahl's Marvellous Medicine* (Liverpool University Press, Liverpool, 2016), p. 55.

5 Ibid.

6 Roald Dahl, 'Zodiac', RDMSC RD2/33/7.

7 Dahl, *Boy*, p. 190.

8 Felicity Dahl, letter to *The Times*, 1990, RDMSC RD 1/6/5.

9 Dahl, *Boy*, p. 206.

10 Dahl, *Going Solo*, pp. 150, 151.

11 See *The Sunday Times*, 4 October 1986.

12 See Levin, *YOU Magazine*, 24 April 1983.

13 Pat Brazier, 'Memories of Roald Dahl', September 2018, RDMSC RD 4/4/40.

14 Dahl, *Going Solo*, p. 210.

15 Ibid., pp. 188–9; Jennet Conant, *The Irregulars* (Simon & Schuster, New York, 2008), p. 16.

16 Tessa Dahl, *Working for Love* (Penguin reprint, London, 1989), p. 5.

17 Dahl, *The Minpins*, p. 92.

18 Sturrock, *Storyteller*, p. 172.

19 Ibid., p. 173.

20 Conant, *The Irregulars*, p. 16.

21 Roald Dahl, Ideas Book 2, RDMSC RD11/2.

22 Dahl, 'Lucky Break', p. 644.

23 Ibid., pp. 641, 642.

24 Ibid., p. 644.

25 Ibid., pp. 644–5.

26 Roald Dahl, 'Shot Down Over Libya', *Saturday Evening Post*, 1 August 1942, p. 38.

27 Dahl, *Boy*, p. 230.

28 Roald Dahl to Professor Brian Cox, Department of Education and Science, 2 June 1988, RDMSC RD2/6/88.

29 Dahl, *Boy*, pp. 223–4.

30 Roald Dahl, *My Uncle Oswald* (Penguin reprint, London, 1980), p. 9.

31 Dahl, *Boy*, p. 227.

32 Ibid.
33 Treglown, *Roald Dahl,* p. 58; Sturrock, *Storyteller,* p. 173.
34 Treglown, *Roald Dahl,* p. 63; Dahl, *My Year,* p. 53.
35 Dahl, *Boy,* p. 226; Dahl, *The Minpins,* pp. 36–7.
36 Sturrock, *Storyteller,* p. 182.
37 Dahl, *Boy,* p. 231.
38 Sturrock, *Love from Boy,* p. 247.
39 Dahl, *Boy,* p. 227.
40 *Kilmarnock Herald & North Ayrshire Gazette,* 17 May 1946.
41 Sturrock, *Storyteller,* p. 176.
42 Ibid., p. 182.
43 Roald Dahl, *The Gremlins* (Walt Disney/Random House, 1943).
44 Sheila St Lawrence to Roald Dahl, 5 June 1957, RDMSC RD1/1/3/282.
45 Dahl, *Boy,* p. 237.
46 Ibid.

Chapter 5: The Perfect Spy?

1 Roald Dahl interview, *Wogan,* BBC1, December 1984.
2 *The Marvellous World of Roald Dahl,* documentary, BBC2, 2016.
3 Roald Dahl to Sofie Magdalene Dahl, 17 June 1943, RDMSC RD14/5/2/19.
4 Ibid., RDMSC RD14/5/2/20; Sturrock, *Storyteller,* p. 228.
5 Sturrock, *Storyteller,* p. 217.
6 Conant, *The Irregulars,* p. 32; William Stephenson to Roald Dahl, 20 June 1945, RDMSC RD15/5/2.
7 Felicity Dahl, in *The Marvellous World of Roald Dahl.*
8 Ibid.

9   Roald Dahl, 'Someone Like You', 1944, reprinted in *The Complete Short Stories Volume One*, p. 186.

10 Felicity Dahl, in *The Marvellous World of Roald Dahl*.

11 Dahl, *Boy*, p. 261.

12 Sturrock, *Storyteller*, p. 319.

13 Dahl, Ideas Book 1; Treglown, *Roald Dahl*, p. 73.

14 Treglown, *Roald Dahl*, p. 53.

15 Ibid., p. 54.

16 Dahl, *My Uncle Oswald*, p. 31; see Sturrock, *Storyteller*, p. 23.

17 Treglown, *Roald Dahl*, pp. 53, 71.

18 Dahl, *Boy*, p. 265; Sturrock, *Storyteller*, p. 232.

19 Dahl, *Boy*, p. 256.

20 Conant, *The Irregulars*, p. 248.

21 Sturrock, *Storyteller*, pp. 228–9.

22 Ibid., p. 336.

23 Roald Dahl, *Boy*, p. 269.

24 Treglown, *Roald Dahl*, p. 73.

25 Ibid., p. 77.

26 Dahl, *Boy*, p. 247.

27 Sturrock, *Storyteller*, p. 273.

28 Dahl, Ideas Book 1.

29 Roald Dahl, 'The Soldier', 1953, reprinted in *The Complete Short Stories Volume One*, p. 477.

30 Sturrock, *Storyteller*, p. 327.

31 Ibid., p. 280.

32 See *The Marvellous World of Roald Dahl*.

33 Dahl, 'Claud's Dog', p. 582.

34 Roald Dahl, notes on 'Mary Honey', RDMSC RD11/3/1/1-8.

35 Roald Dahl to Sofie Magdalene Dahl, 18 March 1951, RDMSC RD14/5/6.

36 Sturrock, *Storyteller*, p. 302.

Chapter 6: My Lady Love, My Dove

1 Roald Dahl, 'My Lady Love, My Dove', 1952, reprinted in *The Complete Short Stories Volume One*, p. 347.

2 Roald Dahl to Sofie Magdalene Dahl, undated, RDMSC RD14/5/6.

3 Roald Dahl to Sofie Magdalene Dahl, 'Thursday evening', undated, RDMSC RD14/5/6; and Roald Dahl to Sofie Magdalene Dahl, 18 December 1951, RDMSC RD14/5/6.

4 Roald Dahl to Sofie Magdalene Dahl, 23 October [1951?], RDMSC RD14/5/6.

5 Roald Dahl to Sofie Magdalene Dahl, 9 May 1951, RDMSC RD14/5/6.

6 Roald Dahl, 'For "The Architectural Digest"', typescript, July 1980, RDMSC RD06020116.

7 Roald Dahl, 'Nunc Dimittis', 1953, reprinted in *The Complete Short Stories Volume One*, p. 370.

8 Felicity and Roald Dahl, *Memories with Food at Gipsy House*, p. 67.

9 Sturrock, *Storyteller*, p. 314.

10 Roald Dahl, 'Mrs Bixby and the Colonel's Coat', 1959, reprinted in *The Complete Short Stories Volume Two*, p. 114.

11 Roald Dahl, 'Princess Mammalia', 1986, reprinted in *The Complete Short Stories Volume Two*, p. 734.

12 Patricia Neal, interviewed in the *Guardian*, 6 January 1971.

13 Sturrock, *Storyteller*, p. 316.

14 Patricia Neal, interviewed in the *Guardian*, 6 January 1971.

15 Sturrock, *Storyteller*, p. 317.

16 Ibid., p. 321.

17 Roald Dahl, speech at Tessa Dahl's wedding, 28 February 1981, RDMSC RD6/1/2/18.

18 See Nadia Cohen, *The Real Roald Dahl* (Pen & Sword, Barnsley, 2018), p. 91.

19 Patricia Neal, interviewed in the *Guardian*, 6 January 1971.

20 Sturrock, *Storyteller*, pp. 332–3.

21 Patricia Neal, interviewed in the *Guardian*, 6 January 1971.

22 Quoted in Solomon, *Roald Dahl's Marvellous Medicine*, pp. 88–9.

23 Roald Dahl, *Charlie and the Great Glass Elevator* (George Allen & Unwin, London, 1973; Puffin reprint *The Complete Adventures of Charlie and Mr Willy Wonka*, 2001), p. 215.

24 Treglown, *Roald Dahl*, p. 115.

25 Dahl, *My Year*, p. 40.

26 Dahl, *Danny the Champion of the World*, p. 107.

27 Tessa Dahl, *Working for Love*, p. 7.

28 Brazier, 'Memories of Roald Dahl'.

29 Dahl, 'For "The Architectural Digest"'.

30 Dahl, *Danny the Champion of the World*, p. 106.

31 Roald Dahl, 'Parson's Pleasure', 1958, reprinted in *The Complete Short Stories Volume Two*, p. 20.

32 *Manchester Evening News*, 29 April 1954.

33 Roald Dahl, 'William and Mary', 1960, reprinted in *The Complete Short Stories Volume Two*, p. 231.

34 Ibid., p. 230.

35 Roald Dahl, 'General Idea for Play in Three Acts', 8 December 1954, RDMSC RD11/3/7.

36 *The Stage*, 7 October 1954.

37 Roald Dahl, 'The Wish', 1953, reprinted in *The Complete Short Stories Volume One*, p. 475.

38 Dahl, *The BFG*, p. 30; Roald Dahl, 'Pig', 1960, reprinted in *The Complete Short Stories Volume Two*, p. 137.

39 Sturrock, *Love from Boy*, p. 96.

40 Patricia Neal, *As I Am* (Simon & Schuster, New York, 1988), p. 190.
41 Sturrock, *Storyteller*, p. 346.
42 See Ian Crouch, 'Roald Dahl's Hut and the Case of the Dippy Adults', *The New Yorker*, 13 September 2011.
43 Alfred Knopf to Roald Dahl, 26 April 1957, RDMSC RD1/1/3/274/1.
44 Roald Dahl, interview, *Pebble Mill at One*, BBC1, 1982.
45 *Aberdeen Evening Express*, 2 June 1960.
46 Roald Dahl, Introduction, *Fear*, p. 11.
47 Ibid., p. 1.
48 Ibid., p. 10.
49 Sheila St Lawrence to Roald Dahl, 27 June 1957, RDMSC RD1/1/3/283.
50 Felicity and Roald Dahl, *Memories with Food at Gipsy House*, p. 226.
51 Else Logsdail (sister), quoted in 'A Dose of Dahl's Magic Medicine'.
52 Dahl, 'For "The Architectural Digest"'.
53 Roald Dahl, 'Goldilocks and the Three Bears', *Revolting Rhymes* (Jonathan Cape, London, 1982).

Chapter 7: Marvellous Medicine

1 Sheila St Lawrence to Roald Dahl, 5 June 1957.
2 Alfred Knopf to Roald Dahl, undated, RDMSC RD1/1/3/274/1.
3 Dahl, Ideas Book 1.
4 Dahl, Ideas Book 2.
5 See RDMSC RD11/3/21/2.
6 See RDMSC RD11/3/11.

7 Sheila St Lawrence to Roald Dahl, see Sturrock, *Storyteller*, p. 364; 'cherry', see RDMSC RD1/1/3/282.

8 Dahl, 'For Children'.

9 Treglown, *Roald Dahl*, p. 124.

10 See RDMSC RD11/3/23/4 and 11/3/23/10.

11 Tessa Dahl, *Working for Love*, p. 19; see Tessa Dahl, 'You Can Love but You'd Better Not Touch', *YOU Magazine*, 1990, RDMSC RD/12/2/11/1.

12 Roald Dahl, 'A Note on Theo's Accident', RDMSC RD11/2.

13 Tessa Dahl, *Working for Love*, p. 28.

14 Solomon, *Roald Dahl's Marvellous Medicine*, p. 84.

15 Ibid., p. 86.

16 Alfhild Hansen (sister), quoted in 'A Dose of Dahl's Magic Medicine'.

17 Roald Dahl to Michael Farmer, undated, RDMSC RD11/1/72.

18 Patricia Neal, *Liverpool Echo*, 7 May 1964.

19 Treglown, *Roald Dahl*, p. 157.

20 Solomon, *Roald Dahl's Marvellous Medicine*, p. 97.

21 Roald Dahl, 'Measles: A Dangerous Illness', open letter written for Sandwell Health Authority, 1986.

22 Roald Dahl, 'Only This', 1944, reprinted in *The Complete Short Stories Volume One*, p. 38.

23 Sturrock, *Storyteller*, p. 388.

24 Tessa Dahl, *Working for Love*, p. 19.

25 Sturrock, *Storyteller*, p. 387.

26 Ibid., p. 391.

27 Solomon, *Roald Dahl's Marvellous Medicine*, p. 106.

28 Roald Dahl, 'Yesterday Was Beautiful', 1945, reprinted in *The Complete Short Stories Volume One*, p. 81.

29 Roald Dahl, *The Missing Golden Ticket* (Puffin, London, 2010), p. 37.

30 Dahl, 'A Note on Writing Books for Children'.
31 Dahl, Ideas Book 1.
32 Roald Dahl to Alfred Knopf, 11 January 1975, see Sturrock, *Storyteller*, p. 470.
33 *Buckinghamshire Examiner*, 10 April 1964.
34 Sturrock, *Storyteller*, p. 407.
35 Treglown, *Roald Dahl*, p. 145.
36 Ibid., p. 148.
37 Roald Dahl to Ray Russell, undated [January/February 1965], private collection.

Chapter 8: Critical Condition

1 *Liverpool Echo*, 20 February 1965.
2 *Daily Telegraph*, 23 February 1965.
3 *Daily Mirror*, 19 February 1965.
4 Felicity and Roald Dahl, *Memories with Food at Gipsy House*, p. 225.
5 Solomon, *Roald Dahl's Marvellous Medicine*, p. 134.
6 Sturrock, *Love from Boy*, p. 289.
7 Solomon, *Roald Dahl's Marvellous Medicine*, p. 139.
8 Blanche Campbell to P. L. Travers, undated [c.1971], private collection.
9 *Liverpool Echo*, 22 May 1965.
10 Solomon, *Roald Dahl's Marvellous Medicine*, p. 140.
11 Sturrock, *Storyteller*, p. 411.
12 Roald Dahl to Sofie Magdalene Dahl, 16 March 1965, RDMSC 14/5/11/12.
13 Sturrock, *Storyteller*, p. 432.
14 Ibid., pp. 420, 416.
15 Ibid., p. 417.
16 Ibid., p. 418.

17 Dahl, *Fantastic Mr Fox*, pp. 19, 77.
18 Sturrock, *Storyteller*, p. 419.
19 Tessa Dahl, *Working for Love*, p. 71; Tessa Dahl, *Daily Mail*, 11 August 2012.
20 Sturrock, *Storyteller*, p. 421.
21 Treglown, *Roald Dahl*, p. 167.
22 Dahl, *The BFG*, p. 45.
23 Treglown, *Roald Dahl*, p. 185.
24 Patricia Neal, interviewed by Peter Lennon, *The Irish Times*, 3 August 1996.
25 Roald Dahl to 'Dear Duke', 15 August 1966, private collection.
26 Treglown, *Roald Dahl*, p. 161.
27 Roald Dahl to Blanche Campbell, 9 June 1967, private collection.
28 See Steven Jay Rubin, *The James Bond Movie Encyclopedia* (Chicago Review Press reprint, 2020).
29 See Roald Dahl, *The Twilight Zone* magazine, February 1983.
30 Roald Dahl to Blanche Campbell, 10 January 1968, private collection.
31 Roald Dahl, *Fantastic Mr Fox*, p. 36.
32 Ibid., p. 77.
33 Ibid., p. 19.
34 Tessa Dahl, *Daily Mail*, 11 August 2012.
35 Ibid.; *New York Post*, 28 July 1973; Solomon, *Roald Dahl's Marvellous Medicine*, p. 171.
36 Treglown, *Roald Dahl*, p. 168.
37 Ibid., p. 174.

Chapter 9: Such Dazzling Loveliness

1 Stephen Michael Shearer, *Patricia Neal: An Unquiet Life* (University Press of Kentucky paperback, 2021), p. 273.
2 Patricia Neal, quoted in *The Australian Women's Weekly*, 15 December 1971.
3 Roald Dahl to Blanche Campbell, 17 October 1971, private collection.
4 Roald Dahl to Robert Newman, undated [*c.*1971], private collection.
5 Dahl, *Charlie and the Chocolate Factory*, pp. 101–2.
6 Dahl, Ideas Book 2.
7 Dahl, *My Uncle Oswald*, p. 89.
8 Tessa Dahl, *Working for Love*, p. 85.
9 Sturrock, *Storyteller*, p. 462.
10 Dahl, *Danny the Champion of the World*, p. 17.
11 Dahl, 'The Author's Eye' notebook, RDMSC.
12 Dahl, *Danny the Champion of the World*, pp. 178–9.
13 Roald Dahl to 'Miss Hoko', Apanui School, Whakatane, New Zealand, 19 June 85.
14 Roald Dahl, *Bedtime Stories* radio interview, 1970.
15 Sturrock, *Storyteller*, p. 470.
16 Roald Dahl, 'The Swan', 1977, reprinted in *The Complete Short Stories Volume Two*, p. 508.
17 Roald Dahl, introduction to 'My Lady Love, My Dove', *Tales of the Unexpected*, series 2, episode 8, 19 April 1980.
18 Dahl, *My Uncle Oswald*, p. 56.
19 Ibid., p. 195.
20 Patricia Neal, *Daily Mirror*, 7 October 1981.
21 Sturrock, *Storyteller*, p. 479.
22 Ibid., p. 497.
23 Dahl, speech at Tessa Dahl's wedding.

24 Tessa Dahl, *Daily Mail*, 11 August 2012.

25 Dahl, speech at Tessa Dahl's wedding.

26 Roald Dahl, *Roald Dahl: In His Own Words*, Radio 4, 2016.

27 Sophie Dahl, in ibid.

28 Roald Dahl, *George's Marvellous Medicine* (Puffin reprint, London, 1982), p. 2.

29 Ibid., p. 103.

30 Sturrock, *Storyteller*, p. 508.

31 Ibid., p. 552.

32 Dahl, *The BFG*, p. 40.

33 Ibid., p. 120.

34 See Levin, *YOU Magazine*, 24 April 1983.

Chapter 10: We So Loved Being With You

1 Roald Dahl to Anna Bingham, 28 January 1985, RDMSC RD1/6/9/2.

2 Dahl, *The Witches*, p. 9.

3 Ibid., p. 189.

4 Dahl, *The Missing Golden Ticket*, p. 59.

5 Roald Dahl to Professor Brian Cox, 2 June 1988, RDMSC RD1/6/13.

6 Roald Dahl, 'The Author's Eye' notebook, RDMSC.

7 Roald Dahl, letter to the editor of *The Times*, 15 September 1983.

8 Sturrock, *Storyteller*, p. 308.

9 Ibid., p. 511.

10 Roald Dahl, letter to the editor of *The Times*, 7 February 1990.

11 Roald Dahl to Angela Levin, 24 April 1983, RDMSC RD12/1/16.

12 Tessa Dahl, 'You Can Love but You'd Better Not Touch'.

13 See the *Observer*, 9 November 2008.

14 Treglown, *Roald Dahl*, p. 235.

15 Sturrock, *Storyteller*, p. 479.

16 Dahl, *The Witches*, pp. 30, 35–6.

17 Dahl, Ideas Book 1.

18 Roald Dahl, 'On Writing *Matilda*', RDMSC RD/6/1/2/30.

19 Dahl, *Matilda*, p. 35.

20 Roald Dahl to Kenneth Baker, 21 November 1988.

21 See Levin, *YOU Magazine*, 24 April 1983.

22 Roald Dahl to Goodrich Community Primary School, East Dulwich, 28 April 1983.

23 Roald Dahl to 'Amy', 10 February 1989, private collection.

24 *The Times*, 27 December 2020.

25 Roald Dahl to Mrs Stafford, undated [1989], RDMSC RD1/6/18.

26 Roald Dahl, Introduction to the Roald Dahl Newsletter, written August 1990, RDMSC RD6/2/1/40.

27 Ibid.

28 Sturrock, *Storyteller*, p. 561.

29 Dahl, 'Dahl Diary'.

30 Felicity Dahl, undated letter [1991], RDMSC RD1/6/10.

31 Tessa Dahl, 'You Can Love but You'd Better Not Touch'.

32 Kiera O' Brien, *The Bookseller*, 22 July 2016.

33 See *Guardian*, 6 November 2018.

34 Mark Kleinman, *Sky News*, 22 September 2021.

35 Dahl, 'Nursery Rhymes'.

Image Credits

Page 1
© Roald Dahl Story Company; © Roald Dahl Story Company;
Walter Attenni/AP/Shutterstock.

Page 2
Shutterstock; Hulton Archive/Getty Images.

Page 3
© Ben Martin.

Page 4
© Dmitri Kasterine.

Page 5
© Ben Martin/Getty Images; PA Images/Alamy;
parkerphotography/Alamy.

Page 6
© Jan Baldwin.

Page 7
© Rob Bogaerts/Anefo/Wikimedia; © Roald Dahl
Story Company.

Page 8
© Roald Dahl Story Company and Quentin Blake (1988);
© Roald Dahl Story Company and Quentin Blake (1982).

Bibliography

The largest collection of archive material relating to the life of Roald Dahl is housed in the Roald Dahl Museum and Story Centre in Great Missenden, Buckinghamshire, where I was helped with great kindness, generosity and good humour by archivist and collections manager Rachel White.

Cohen, Nadia, *The Real Roald Dahl* (Pen & Sword, Barnsley, 2018)

Conant, Jennet, *The Irregulars: Roald Dahl and the British Spy Ring in Wartime Washington* (Simon & Schuster, New York, 2008)

Crommelin-Brown, John, *Dies Heroica* (Hodder & Stoughton, London, 1918)

Crouch, Ian, 'Roald Dahl's Hut and the Case of the Dippy Adults', *The New Yorker*, September 2011

Dahl, Tessa, *Working for Love* (Penguin reprint, London, 1989)

Farrell, Barry, *Pat and Roald* (Hutchinson, London, 1970)

Keene, Alice, *The Two Mr Smiths: The Life and Work of Sir Matthew Smith* (Lund Humphries paperback, London, 1995)

Kopper, Philip, *Anonymous Giver: A Life of Charles E. Marsh* (Public Welfare Foundation, Washington DC, 2000)

Maschler, Tom, *Publisher* (Picador, London, 2005)

Murray Levick, George, *Journal of the Royal Society of Arts*, 4 August 1939

Neal, Patricia, *As I Am* (Simon & Schuster, New York, 1988)

NSPCC, *When We Were Young: Memories of Childhood* (David & Charles, Newton Abbot, 1987)

Rosen, Michael, *Fantastic Mr Dahl* (Puffin, London, 2012)

Rubin, Steven Jay, *The James Bond Movie Encyclopedia* (Chicago Review Press reprint, 2020)

Shearer, Stephen Michael, *Patricia Neal: An Unquiet Life* (University Press of Kentucky, 2006)

Sturrock, Donald, *Storyteller: The Life of Roald Dahl* (Harper Press paperback, London, 2011)

Sturrock, Donald, *Love from Boy: Roald Dahl's Letters to his Mother* (John Murray, London, 2016)

Travers, P. L., 'Johnny Delaney', 1944, included in *Aunt Sass Christmas Stories* (Virago, London, 2014)

Treglown, Jeremy, *Roald Dahl: A Biography* (Faber and Faber, London, 1994)

Treglown, Jeremy, 'The Fantastic Mr Dahl', *Smithsonian Magazine*, July 2016

Walford Davies, Damian, ed., *Roald Dahl: Wales of the Unexpected* (University of Wales Press, Cardiff, 2016)

Index

INDEX

257